THE BEST OF J. C. RYLE

In memory of
Jessie, Mary and Kate Macgillivray
whose love for the Lord Jesus produced in them a
deep and lasting appreciation of Christian literature,
and a desire that many share such a privilege.

W. J. C. and J.C.

THE BEST
OF
J. C. RYLE

A treasury of extracts from
the writings of J. C. Ryle

CHRISTIAN FOCUS PUBLICATIONS

© 1981 Baker Book House
Published in the USA by Baker Book House Co.,
Grand Rapids, Michigan

This British edition
published in
1991
by
Christian Focus Publications Ltd
Geanies House, Fearn IV20 1TW
Ross-shire, Scotland, UK.

ISBN 1 871 676 649

Cover design
by
Seoris McGillivray

Printed & bound in Great Britain by
Cox & Wyman Ltd, Reading.

Contents

1

Sin

"Sin is the transgression of the law."—John 3:4

He that wishes to attain right views about Christian holiness, must begin by examining the vast and solemn subject of *sin*. He must dig down very low if he would build high. A mistake here is most mischievous. Wrong views about holiness are generally traceable to wrong views about human corruption. I make no apology for beginning this volume of papers about holiness by making some plain statements about *sin*.

The plain truth is that a right knowledge of sin lies at the root of all saving Christianity. Without it such doctrines as justification, conversion, sanctification, are "words and names" which convey no meaning to the mind. The first thing, therefore, that God does when He makes any one a new creature in Christ, is to send light into his heart, and show him that he is a guilty sinner. The material creation in Genesis began with "light," and so also does the spiritual creation. God "shines into our hearts" by the work of the Holy Ghost, and then spiritual life begins (II Cor. 4:6). Dim or indistinct views of sin are the origin of most of the errors,

1

heresies, and false doctrines of the present day. If a man does not realize the dangerous nature of his soul's disease, you cannot wonder if he is content with false or imperfect remedies. I believe that one of the chief wants of the church in the nineteenth century has been, and is, clearer, fuller teaching about sin.

(1) I shall begin the subject by supplying some DEFINITION of sin. We are all of course familiar with the terms "sin" and "sinners." We talk frequently of "sin" being in the world, and of men committing "sins." But what do we mean by these terms and phrases? Do we really know? I fear there is much mental confusion and haziness on this point. Let me try, as briefly as possible, to supply an answer.

I say, then, that "sin," speaking generally, is, as the ninth article of our church declares, "the fault and corruption of the nature of every man that is naturally engendered of the offspring of Adam; whereby man is very far gone (*quam longissimè* is the Latin) from original righteousness, and is of his own nature inclined to evil, so that the flesh lusteth alway against the spirit; and, therefore, in every person born into the world, it deserveth God's wrath and damnation." Sin, in short, is that vast moral disease which affects the whole human race, of every rank, and class, and name, and nation, and people, and tongue; a disease from which there never was but one born of woman that was free. Need I say that one was Christ Jesus the Lord?

I say, furthermore, that "a sin," to speak more particularly, consists in doing, saying, thinking, or imagining, anything that is not in perfect conformity with the mind and law of God. "Sin," in short, as the Scripture saith, is "the transgression of the law" (I John 3:4). The slightest outward or inward departure from absolute mathematical parallelism with God's revealed will and character constitutes a sin, and at once makes us guilty in God's sight.

Of course I need not tell any one who reads his Bible with attention, that a man may break God's law in heart and thought, when there is no overt and visible act of wickedness. Our Lord has settled that point beyond dispute in the Sermon on the Mount (Matt. 5:21–28). Even a poet of our own has truly said, "A man may smile and smile, and be a villain."

Again, I need not tell a careful student of the New Testament, that there are sins of omission as well as commission, and that we sin, as our Prayerbook justly reminds us, by "leaving undone the things we ought to do," as really as by "doing the things we ought not to do." The solemn words of our Master in the Gospel of St. Matthew place this point also beyond dispute. It is there written, "Depart from me, ye cursed, into everlasting fire . . . for I was an hungered, and ye gave me no meat; I was thirsty, and ye gave me no drink" (Matt. 25:41, 42). It was a deep and thoughtful saying of the holy Archbishop Ussher, just before he died, "Lord, forgive me all my sins, and specially my sins of omission."

But I do think it necessary in these times to remind my readers that a man may commit sin and yet be ignorant of it, and fancy himself innocent when he is guilty. I fail to see any scriptural warrant for the modern assertion that "Sin is not sin to us until we discern it and are conscious of it." On the contrary, in the fourth and fifth chapters of that unduly neglected book, Leviticus, and in the fifteenth of Numbers, I find Israel distinctly taught that there were sins of *ignorance* which rendered people unclean, and needed atonement (Lev. 4:1–35; 5:14–19; Num. 15:25–29). And I find our Lord expressly teaching that "the servant who knew not his master's will and did it not" was not excused on account of his ignorance, but was "beaten" or punished (Luke 12:48). We shall do well to remember, that when we make our own miserably imperfect knowledge and consciousness the measure of our sinfulness, we are on very dangerous ground. A deeper study of Leviticus might do us much good.

(2) Concerning the ORIGIN AND SOURCE of this vast moral disease called "sin" I must say something. I fear the views of many professing Christians on this point are sadly defective and unsound. I dare not pass it by. Let us, then, have it fixed down in our minds that the sinfulness of man does not begin from without, but from within. It is not the result of bad training in early years. It is not picked up from bad companions and bad examples, as some weak Christians are too fond of saying. No! it is a family disease, which we all inherit from our first parents, Adam and Eve, and with which we are born. Created "in the image of God," innocent and righteous at first, our parents fell from original righteousness and became sinful and corrupt. And from that day to this all men and women are born in the image of fallen Adam and Eve, and inherit a heart and nature inclined to evil. "By one man sin entered into the world." "That which is born of the flesh is flesh." "We are by nature children of wrath." "The carnal mind is enmity against God." "Out of the heart [naturally as out of a fountain] proceed evil thoughts, adulteries," and the like (John 3:6; Eph. 2:3; Rom. 8:7; Mark 7:21). The fairest babe that has entered life this year, and become the sunbeam of a family, is not, as its mother perhaps fondly calls it, a little "angel," or a little "innocent," but a little "sinner." Alas, as it lies smiling and crowing in its cradle, that little creature carries in its heart the seeds of every kind of wickedness! Only watch it carefully, as it grows in stature and its mind develops, and you will soon detect in it an incessant tendency to that which is

bad, and a backwardness to that which is good. You will see in it the buds and germs of deceit, evil temper, selfishness, self-will, obstinacy, greediness, envy, jealousy, passion—which, if indulged and let alone, will shoot up with painful rapidity. Who taught the child these things? Where did he learn them? The Bible alone can answer these questions! Of all the foolish things that parents say about their children there is none worse than the common saying, "My son *has a good heart at the bottom*. He is not what he ought to be; but he has fallen into bad hands. Public schools are bad places. The tutors neglect the boys. Yet he has a good heart at the bottom." The truth, unhappily, is diametrically the other way. The first cause of all sin lies in the natural corruption of the boy's own heart, and not in the school.

(3) Concerning the EXTENT of this vast moral disease of man called sin, let us beware that we make no mistake. The only safe ground is that which is laid for us in Scripture. "Every imagination of the thoughts of his heart" is by nature "evil, and that continually." "The heart is deceitful above all things, and desperately wicked" (Gen. 6:5; Jer. 17:9). Sin is a disease which pervades and runs through every part of our moral constitution and every faculty of our minds. The understanding, the affections, the reasoning powers, the will, are all more or less infected. Even the conscience is so blinded that it cannot be depended on as a sure guide, and is as likely to lead men wrong as right, unless it is enlightened by the Holy Ghost. In short, "from the sole of the foot even unto the head there is no soundness" about us (Isa. 1:6). The disease may be veiled under a thin covering of courtesy, politeness, good manners, and outward decorum; but it lies deep down in the constitution.

I admit fully that man has many grand and noble faculties left about him, and that in arts and sciences and literature he shows immense capacity. But the fact still remains that in spiritual things he is utterly "dead," and has no natural knowledge, or love, or fear of God. His best things are so interwoven and intermingled with corruption, that the contrast only brings out into sharper relief the truth and extent of *the fall*. That one and the same creature should be in some things so high and in others so low, so great and yet so little, so noble and yet so mean, so grand in his conception and execution of material things, and yet so groveling and debased in his affections, that he should be able to plan and erect buildings like those to Carnac and Luxor in Egypt, and the Parthenon at Athens, and yet worship vile gods and goddesses, and birds, and beasts, and creeping things, that he should be able to produce tragedies like those of Aeschylus and Sophocles, and histories like that of Thucydides, and yet be a slave to abominable vices like those described in the first chapter of the Epistle to the Romans—all this is a sore puzzle to those who sneer at "God's Word written," and scoff at us as bibliolaters. But it is a knot that we can untie with the Bible in our hands. We can acknowledge that man has all the marks of a majestic temple about him, a temple in which God once dwelt, but a temple which is now in utter ruins, a temple in which a shattered window here, and a doorway there, and a column there, still give some faint idea of the magnificence of the original design, but a temple which from end to end has lost its glory and fallen from its high estate. And we say that nothing solves the complicated problem of man's condition but the doctrine of original or birth-sin and the crushing effects of the fall.

Let us remember, beside this, that every part of the world bears testimony to the fact that sin is the *universal disease of all mankind*. Search the globe from east to west and from pole to pole, search every nation of every clime in the four quarters of the earth, search every rank and class in our own country from the highest to the lowest—and under every circumstance and condition, the report will always be the same. The remotest islands in the Pacific Ocean, completely separate from Europe, Asia, Africa, and America, beyond the reach alike of Oriental luxury and Western arts and literature, islands inhabited by people ignorant of books, money, steam, and gunpowder, uncontaminated by the vices of modern civilization—these very islands have always been found, when first discovered, the abode of the vilest forms of lust, cruelty, deceit, and superstition. If the inhabitants have known nothing else, they have always known how to sin! Everywhere the human heart is naturally "deceitful above all things, and desperately wicked" (Jer. 17:9). For my part, I know no stronger proof of the inspiration of Genesis and the Mosaic account of the origin of man, than the power, extent, and universality of sin. Grant that mankind have all sprung from one pair, and that this pair fell (as Gen. 3 tells us), and the state of human nature everywhere is easily accounted for. Deny it, as many do, and you are at once involved in inexplicable difficulties. In a word, the uniformity and universality of human corruption supply one of the most unanswerable instances of the enormous "difficulties of infidelity."

After all, I am convinced that the greatest proof of the extent and power of sin is the pertinacity with which it cleaves to man, even after he is converted and has become the subject of the Holy Ghost's operations. To use the language of the ninth article, "this infection of nature doth remain—yea, even in them that are regenerate." So deeply planted are the roots of human corruption, that even after we are born again, renewed, "washed, sanctified, justified," and made living members of Christ, these roots remain alive in the bottom of our hearts, and, like the leprosy in the walls of the house, we never get rid of them until the earthly house of this tabernacle is dissolved. Sin, no doubt, in the believer's heart, has no longer *dominion*. It is checked, controlled, mortified, and crucified by the expulsive power of the new principle of grace. The life of a believer is a life of victory, and not of failure. But the very struggles which go on within his bosom, the fight that he finds it needful to fight daily, the watchful jealousy which he is obliged to exercise over his inner man, the contest between the flesh and the spirit, the inward "groanings" which no one knows but he who has experienced them—all, all testify to the same great truth. All show the enormous power and vitality of sin. Mighty indeed must that foe be who even when crucified is still alive! Happy is that believer who understands it, and while he rejoices in Christ Jesus has no confidence in the flesh; and while he says, "Thanks be unto God who giveth us the victory," never forgets to watch and pray lest he fall into temptation!

(4) Concerning the GUILT, VILENESS, and OFFENSIVENESS of sin in the sight of God, my words shall be few. I say "few" advisedly. I do not think, in the nature of things, that mortal man can at all realize the exceeding sinfulness of sin in the sight of that holy and perfect one with whom we have to do. On the one hand, God is that eternal being who "chargeth his angels with folly," and in whose sight the very "heavens are not clean." He is one who reads thoughts and motives as well as actions, and requires "truth in the inward parts" (Job 4:18; 15:15; Ps. 51:6). We, on the other hand—poor blind creatures, here today and gone tomorrow, born in sin, surrounded by sinners, living in a constant atmosphere of weakness, infirmity, and imperfection—can form none but the most inadequate conceptions of the hideousness of evil.

We have no line to fathom it, and no measure by which to gauge it. The blind man can see no difference between a masterpiece of Titian or Raphael, and the Queen's Head on a village signboard. The deaf man cannot distinguish between a penny whistle and a cathedral organ. The very animals whose smell is most offensive to us have no idea that they are offensive, and are not offensive to one another. And man, fallen man, I believe, can have no just idea what a vile thing sin is in the sight of that God whose handiwork is absolutely perfect, perfect whether we look through telescope or microscope, perfect in the formation of a mighty planet like Jupiter, with his satellites, keeping time to a second as he rolls round the sun, perfect in the formation of the smallest insect that crawls over a foot of ground. But let us nevertheless settle it firmly in our minds that sin is "the abominable thing that God hateth"; that God "is of purer eyes than to behold iniquity, and cannot look upon that which is evil"; that the least transgression of God's law makes us "guilty of all"; that "the soul that sinneth shall die"; that "the wages of sin is death"; that God shall "judge the secrets of men"; that there is a worm that never dies, and a fire that is not quenched; that "the wicked shall be turned into hell" and "shall go away into everlasting punishment"; and that "nothing that defiles shall in any wise enter" heaven (Jer. 44:4; Hab. 1:13; James 2:10; Ezek. 18:4; Rom. 6:23; Rom. 2:16; Mark 9:44; Ps. 9:17; Matt. 25:46; Rev. 21:27). These are indeed tremendous words, when we consider that they are written in the Book of a most merciful God!

No proof of the fullness of sin, after all, is so overwhelming and unanswerable as the cross and passion of our Lord Jesus Christ, and the whole doctrine of His substitution and atonement. Terribly black must that guilt be for which nothing but the blood of the Son of God could make satisfaction. Heavy must that weight of human sin be which made Jesus groan and sweat drops of blood in agony at Gethsemane, and cry at Golgotha, "My God, my God, why hast thou forsaken me?" (Matt. 27:46). Nothing, I am convinced, will astonish us so much, when we awake in the resurrection day, as the view we shall have of sin, and the retrospect we shall take of our own countless shortcomings and defects. Never till the hour when Christ comes the second time shall we fully realize the "sinfulness of sin." Well might George Whitefield say, "The anthem in heaven will be, What hath God wrought!"

(5) One point only remains to be considered on the subject of sin, which I dare not pass over. That point is its DECEITFULNESS. It is a point of most serious importance, and I venture to think it does not receive the attention which it deserves. You may see this deceitfulness in the wonderful proneness of men to regard sin as less sinful and dangerous than it is in the sight of God; and in their readiness to extenuate it, make excuses for it, and minimize its guilt. "It is but a little one! God is merciful! God is not extreme to mark what is done amiss! We mean well! One cannot be so particular! Where is the mighty harm? We only do as others!" Who is not familiar with this kind of language? You may see it in the long string of smooth words and phrases which men have coined in order to designate things which God calls downright wicked and ruinous to the soul. What do such expressions as "fast," "gay," "wild," "unsteady," "thoughtless," "loose" mean? They show that men try to cheat themselves into the belief that sin is not quite so sinful as God says it is, and that they are not so bad as they really are. You may see it in the tendency even of believers to indulge their children in

questionable practices, and to blind their own eyes to the inevitable result of the love of money, of tampering with temptation, and sanctioning a low standard of family religion. I fear we do not sufficiently realize the extreme subtlety of our soul's disease. We are too apt to forget that temptation to sin will rarely present itself to us in its true colors, saying, "I am your deadly enemy, and I want to ruin you for ever in hell." Oh, no, sin comes to us, like Judas, with a kiss; and like Joab, with an outstretched hand and flattering words. The forbidden fruit seemed good and desirable to Eve; yet it cast her out of Eden. The walking idly on his palace roof seemed harmless enough to David; yet it ended in adultery and murder. Sin rarely seems sin at its first beginnings. Let us then watch and pray, lest we fall into temptation. We may give wickedness smooth names, but we cannot alter its nature and character in the sight of God. Let us remember St. Paul's words: "Exhort one another daily, lest any be hardened through the deceitfulness of sin" (Heb. 3:13). It is a wise prayer in our litany, "From the *deceits* of the world, the flesh, and the devil, good Lord, deliver us."

And now, before I go further, let me briefly mention two thoughts which appear to me to rise with irresistible force out of the subject.

On the one hand, I ask my readers to observe what deep reasons we all have *for humiliation and self-abasement.* Let us sit down before the picture of sin displayed to us in the Bible, and consider what guilty, vile, corrupt creatures we all are in the sight of God. What need we all have of that entire change of heart called regeneration, new birth, or conversion! What a mass of infirmity and imperfection cleaves to the very best of us at our very best! What a solemn thought it is, that "without holiness no man shall see the Lord"! (Heb. 12:14). What cause we have to cry with the publican, every night in our lives, when we think of our sins of omission as well as commission, ''God be merciful to me a sinner''! (Luke 18:13). How admirably suited are the general and communion confessions of the Prayerbook to the actual condition of all professing Christians! How well that language which the Prayerbook puts in the mouth of every Churchman before he goes up to the communion table suits God's children—''The remembrance of our misdoings is grievous unto us; the burden is intolerable. Have mercy upon us, have mercy upon us, most merciful Father; for Thy Son our Lord Jesus Christ's sake, forgive us all that is past.'' How true it is that the holiest saint is in himself a miserable sinner,'' and a debtor to mercy and grace to the last moment of his existence!

With my whole heart I subscribe to that passage in Hooker's sermon on justification, which begins,

Let the holiest and best things we do be considered. We are never better affected unto God than when we pray; yet when we pray, how are our affections many times distracted! How little reverence do we show unto the grand majesty of God unto whom we speak! How little remorse of our own miseries! How little taste of the sweet influence of His tender mercies do we feel! Are we not as unwilling many times to begin, and as glad to make an end, as if in saying, ''Call upon Me,'' He had set us a very burdensome task? It may seem somewhat extreme, which I will speak; therefore, let every one judge of it, even as his own heart shall tell him, and not otherwise; I will but only make a demand! If God should yield unto us, not as unto Abraham,—If fifty, forty, thirty, twenty—yea, or if ten good persons could be found in a city, for their sakes this city should not be destroyed; but, and if He should make us an offer thus large, Search all the generations of men since the fall of our father Adam, find one man that hath done one action which hath passed from him pure, without any

stain or blemish at all; and for that one man's only action neither man nor angel should feel the torments
which are prepared for both. Do you think that this ran-
som to deliver men and angels could be found to be
among the sons of men? The best things which we do
have somewhat in them to be pardoned.

That witness is true. For my part I am persuaded the
more light we have, the more we see our own sinfulness;
the nearer we get to heaven, the more we are clothed
with humility. In every age of the church you will find it
true, if you will study biographies, that the most eminent saints—men like Bradford, Rutherford, and Mc-
Cheyne—have always been the humblest men.

On the other hand, I ask my readers to observe *how
deeply thankful we ought to be for the glorious gospel of
the grace of God.* There is a remedy revealed for man's
need, as wide and broad and deep as man's disease. We
need not be afraid to look at sin, and study its nature,
origin, power, extent, and vileness, if we only look at the
same time at the almighty medicine provided for us in
the salvation that is in Jesus Christ. Though sin has
abounded, grace has much more abounded. Yes, in the
everlasting covenant of redemption, to which Father,
Son, and Holy Ghost are parties, in the mediator of that
covenant, Jesus Christ the righteous, perfect God and
perfect man in one person, in the work that He did by
dying for our sins and rising again for our justification,
in the offices that He fills as our priest, substitute, physician, shepherd, and advocate, in the precious blood He
shed which can cleanse from all sin, in the everlasting
righteousness that He brought, in the perpetual intercession that He carries on as our representative at God's
right hand, in His power to save to the uttermost the
chief of sinners, His willingness to receive and pardon
the vilest, His readiness to bear with the weakest, in the

grace of the Holy Spirit which He plants in the hearts of all His people, renewing, sanctifying, and causing old things to pass away and all things to become new—in all this—and oh, what a brief sketch it is!—in all this, I say, there is a full, perfect, and complete medicine for the hideous disease of sin. Awful and tremendous as the right view of sin undoubtedly is, no one need faint and despair if he will take a right view of Jesus Christ at the same time. No wonder that old Flavel ends many a chapter of his admirable "Fountain of Life" with the touching words, "Blessed be God for Jesus Christ."

In bringing this mighty subject to a close, I feel that I have only touched the surface of it. It is one which cannot be thoroughly handled in a paper like this. He that would see it treated fully and exhaustively must turn to such masters of experimental theology as Owen, and Burgess, and Manton, and Charnock, and the other giants of the Puritan school. On subjects like this there are no writers to be compared to the Puritans. It only remains for me to point out some practical uses to which the whole doctrine of sin may be profitably turned in the present day.

(a) I say, then, in the first place, that a scriptural view of sin is one of the *best antidotes to that vague, dim, misty, hazy kind of theology* which is so painfully current in the present age. It is vain to shut our eyes to the fact that there is a vast quantity of so-called Christianity now-a-days which you cannot declare positively unsound, but which, nevertheless, is not full measure, good weight, and sixteen ounces to the pound. It is a Christianity in which there is undeniably "something about Christ, and something about grace, and something about faith, and something about repentance, and something about holiness"; but it is not the real "thing as it is" in the Bible. Things are out of place, and out of proportion. As old Latimer would have said, it is a kind of "mingle-mangle," and does no good. It neither exercises influence on daily conduct, nor comforts in life, nor gives peace in death; and those who hold it often awake too late to find that they have got nothing solid under their feet. Now I believe the likeliest way to cure and mend this defective kind of religion is to bring forward more prominently the old scriptural truth about the sinfulness of sin. People will never set their faces decidedly towards heaven, and live like pilgrims, until they really feel that they are in danger of hell. Let us all try to revive the old teaching about sin, in nurseries, in schools, in training colleges, in universities. Let us not forget that "the law is good if we use it lawfully," and that "by the law is the knowledge of sin" (I Tim. 1:8; Rom. 3:20; 7:7). Let us bring the law to the front and press it on men's attention. Let us expound and beat out the Ten Commandments, and show the length, and breadth, and depth, and height of their requirements. This is the way of our Lord in the Sermon on the Mount. We cannot do better than follow His plan. We may depend upon it, men will never come to Jesus, and stay with Jesus, and live for Jesus, unless they really know why they are to come, and what is their need. Those whom the Spirit draws to Jesus are those whom the Spirit has convinced of sin. Without thorough conviction of sin, men may seem to come to Jesus and follow Him for a season, but they will soon fall away and return to the world.

(b) In the next place, a scriptural view of sin is one of the *best antidotes to the extravagantly broad and liberal theology* which is so much in vogue at the present time. The tendency of modern thought is to reject dogmas, creeds, and every kind of bounds in religion. It is thought grand and wise to condemn no opinion whatso-

ever, and to pronounce all earnest and clever teachers to be trustworthy, however heterogeneous and mutually destructive their opinions may be. Everything forsooth is true, and nothing is false! Everybody is right, and nobody is wrong! Everybody is likely to be saved, and nobody is to be lost? The atonement and substitution of Christ, the personality of the devil, the miraculous element in Scripture, the reality and eternity of future punishment, all these mighty foundation-stones are coolly tossed overboard, like lumber, in order to lighten the ship of Christianity, and enable it to keep pace with modern science. Stand up for these great verities, and you are called narrow, illiberal, old-fashioned, and a theological fossil! Quote a text, and you are told that all truth is not confined to the pages of an ancient Jewish book, and that free inquiry has found out many things since the book was completed! Now, I know nothing so likely to counteract this modern plague as constant clear statements about the nature, reality, vileness, power, and guilt of sin. We must charge home into the consciences of these men of *broad* views, and demand a plain answer to some plain questions. We must ask them to lay their hands on their hearts, and tell us whether their favorite opinions comfort them in the day of sickness, in the hour of death, by the bedside of dying parents, by the grave of beloved wife or child. We must ask them whether a vague *earnestness,* without definite doctrine, gives them peace at seasons like these. We must challenge them to tell us whether they do not sometimes feel a gnawing ''something'' within, which all the free inquiry and philosophy and science in the world cannot satisfy. And then we must tell them that this gnawing ''something'' is the sense of sin, guilt, and corruption, which they are leaving out in their calculations. And, above all, we must tell them that nothing will ever make them feel rest, but submission to the old doctrines of man's ruin and Christ's redemption, and simple child-like faith in Jesus.

(c) In the next place, a right view of sin is the *best antidote to that sensuous, ceremonial, formal kind of Christianity*, which has swept over England like a flood in the last twenty-five years, and carried away so many before it. I can well believe that there is much that is attractive in this system of religion, to a certain order of minds, so long as the conscience is not fully enlightened. But when that wonderful part of our constitution called conscience is really awake and alive, I find it hard to believe that a sensuous, ceremonial Christianity will thoroughly satisfy us. A little child is easily quieted and amused with gaudy toys, and dolls, and rattles, so long as it is not hungry; but once let it feel the cravings of nature within, and we know that nothing will satisfy it but *food*. Just so it is with man in the matter of his soul. Music, and flowers, and candles, and incense, and banners, and processions, and beautiful vestments, and confessionals, and manmade ceremonies of a semi-Romish character, may do well enough for him under certain conditions. But once let him "awake and arise from the dead," and he will not rest content with these things. They will seem to him mere solemn triflings, and a waste of time. Once let him see his *sin*, and he must see his *Savior*. He feels stricken with a deadly disease, and nothing will satisfy him but the great physician. He hungers and thirsts, and he must have nothing less than the bread of life. I may seem bold in what I am about to say; but I fearlessly venture the assertion, that four-fifths of the semi-Romanism of the last quarter of a century would never have existed if English people had been taught more fully and clearly the nature, vileness, and sinfulness of sin.

(d) In the next place, a right view of sin is one of the *best antidotes to the overstrained theories of perfection*, of which we hear so much in these times. I shall say but little about this, and in saying it I trust I shall not give offense. If those who press on us perfection mean nothing more than an all-round consistency, and a careful attention to all the graces which make up the Christian character, reason would that we should not only bear with them, but agree with them entirely. By all means let us aim high. But if men really mean to tell us that here in this world a believer can attain to entire freedom from sin, live for years in unbroken and uninterrupted communion with God, and feel for months together not so much as one evil thought, I must honestly say·that such an opinion appears to me very *unscriptural*. I go even further. I say that the opinion is very dangerous to him that holds it, and very likely to depress, discourage, and keep back inquirers after salvation. I cannot find the slightest warrant in God's Word for expecting such perfection as this while we are in the body. I believe the words of our fifteenth article are strictly true, that "Christ alone is without sin; and that all we, the rest, though baptized and born again in Christ, offend in many things; and if we say that we have no sin we deceive ourselves and the truth is not in us." To use the language of our first homily, "There be imperfections in our best works: we do not love God so much as we are bound to do, with all our heart, mind, and power; we do not fear God so much as we ought to do; we do not pray to God but with many and great imperfections. We give, forgive, believe, live, and hope imperfectly; we speak, think, and do imperfectly; we fight against the devil, the world, and the flesh imperfectly. Let us, therefore, not be ashamed to confess plainly our state of imperfection." Once more I repeat what I have said, the

best preservative against this temporary delusion about perfection which clouds some minds—for such I hope I may call it—is a clear, full, distinct understanding of the nature, sinfulness, and deceitfulness of sin.

(e) In the last place, a scriptural view of sin will prove an admirable *antidote to the low views of personal holiness,* which are so painfully prevalent in these last days of the church. This is a very painful and delicate subject, I know; but I dare not turn away from it. It has long been my sorrowful conviction that the standard of daily life among professing Christians in this country has been gradually falling. I am afraid that Christlike charity, kindness, good temper, unselfishness, meekness, gentleness, good nature, self-denial, zeal to do good, and separation from the world, are far less appreciated than they ought to be, and than they used to be in the days of our fathers.

Into the causes of this state of things I cannot pretend to enter fully, and can only suggest conjectures for consideration. It may be that a certain profession of religion has become so fashionable and comparatively easy in the present age, that the streams which were once narrow and deep have become wide and shallow, and what we have gained in outward show we have lost in quality. It may be that the vast increase of wealth in the last twenty-five years has insensibly introduced a plague of worldliness, and self-indulgence, and love of ease into social life. What were once called luxuries are now comforts and necessaries, and self-denial and "enduring hardness" are consequently little known. It may be that the enormous amount of controversy which marks this age has insensibly dried up our spiritual life. We have too often been content with zeal for orthodoxy, and have neglected the sober realities of daily practical godliness. Be the causes what they may, I must declare my own belief that the result remains. There has been of late years a lower standard of personal holiness among believers than there used to be in the days of our fathers. The whole result is that THE SPIRIT IS GRIEVED! and the matter calls for much humiliation and searching of heart.

As to the best remedy for the state of things I have mentioned, I shall venture to give an opinion. Other schools of thought in the churches must judge for themselves. The cure for evangelical churchmen, I am convinced, is to be found in a clearer apprehension of the nature and sinfulness of sin. We need not go back to Egypt, and borrow semi-Romish practices in order to revive our spiritual life. We need not restore the confessional, or return to monasticism or asceticism. Nothing of the kind! We must simply repent and do our first works. We must return to first principles. We must go back to "the old paths." We must sit down humbly in the presence of God, look the whole subject in the face, examine clearly what the Lord Jesus calls sin, and what the Lord Jesus calls "doing his will." We must then try to realize that it is *terribly possible* to live a careless, easygoing, half-worldly life, and yet at the same time to maintain evangelical principles and call ourselves evangelical people! Once let us see that sin is far viler, and far nearer to us, and sticks more closely to us than we supposed, and we shall be led, I trust and believe, to get nearer to Christ. Once drawn nearer to Christ, we shall drink more deeply out of His fullness, and learn more thoroughly to "live the life of faith" in Him, as St. Paul did. Once taught to live the life of faith in Jesus, and abiding in Him, we shall bear more fruit, shall find ourselves more strong for duty, more patient in trial, more watchful over our poor weak hearts, and more like our Master in all our little daily ways. Just in proportion as we realize how much Christ has done for us, shall we labor to do much for Christ. Much forgiven, we shall love much. In short, as the apostle says, "with open face beholding as in a glass the glory of the Lord, we are changed into the same image even as by the Spirit of the Lord" (II Cor. 3:18).

Whatever some may please to think or say, there can be no doubt that an increased feeling about holiness is one of the signs of the times. Conferences for the promotion of "spiritual life" are becoming common in the present day. The subject of "spiritual life" finds a place on congress platforms almost every year. It has awakened an amount of interest and general attention throughout the land, for which we ought to be thankful. Any movement, based on sound principles, which helps to deepen our spiritual life and increase our personal holiness, will be a real blessing to the Church of England. It will do much to draw us together and heal our unhappy divisions. It may bring down some fresh outpouring of the grace of the Spirit, and be "life from the dead" in these later times. But sure I am, as I said in the beginning of this paper, we must begin low, if we would build high. I am convinced that the first step towards attaining a higher standard of holiness is to realize more fully the amazing sinfulness of sin.

2

Holiness

"Holiness, without which no man shall see the Lord."—Heb. 12:14

The text which heads this page opens up a subject of deep importance. That subject is practical holiness. It suggests a question which demands the attention of all professing Christians, Are we holy? Shall we see the Lord?

That question can never be out of season. The wise man tells us, "There is a time to weep, and a time to laugh . . . a time to keep silence, and a time to speak" (Eccles. 3:4, 7); but there is no time, no, not a day, in which a man ought not to be holy. Are we?

That question concerns all ranks and conditions of men. Some are rich and some are poor, some learned and some unlearned, some masters and some servants; but there is no rank or condition in life in which a man ought not to be holy. Are we?

I ask to be heard today about this question. How stands the account between our souls and God? In this hurrying, bustling world, let us stand still for a few minutes and consider the matter of holiness. I believe I might have chosen a subject more popular and pleasant. I am sure I might have found one more easy to handle. But I feel deeply I could not have chosen one more seasonable and more profitable to our souls. It is a solemn thing to hear the Word of God saying, "Without holiness no man shall see the Lord" (Heb. 12:14).

I shall endeavor, by God's help, to examine what true holiness is, and the reason why it is so needful. In conclusion, I shall try to point out the only way in which holiness can be attained. I have already, in the second paper in this volume, approached this subject from a doctrinal side. Let me now try to present it to my readers in a more plain and practical point of view.

I. First then, let me try to show *what true practical holiness is—what sort of persons are those whom God calls holy.*

A man may go great lengths, and yet never reach true holiness. It is not knowledge—Balaam had that; nor great profession—Judas Iscariot had that; nor doing many things—Herod had that; nor zeal for certain matters in religion—Jehu had that; nor morality and outward respectability of conduct—the young ruler had that; nor taking pleasure in hearing preachers—the Jews in Ezekiel's time had that; nor keeping company with godly people—Joab and Gehazi and Demas had that. Yet none of these were holy! These things alone are not holiness. A man may have any one of them, and yet never see the Lord.

What then is true practical holiness? It is a hard question to answer. I do not mean that there is any want of scriptural matter on the subject. But I fear lest I should give a defective view of holiness, and not say all that ought to be said; or lest I should say things about it that ought not to be said, and so do harm. Let me, however, try to draw a picture of holiness, that we may see it clearly before the eyes of our minds. Only let it never be forgotten, when I have said all, that my account is but a poor imperfect outline at the best.

(a) Holiness is *the habit of being of one mind with God,* according as we find His mind described in Scripture. It is the habit of agreeing in God's judgment—hating what He hates, loving what He loves, and measuring everything in this world by the standard of His Word. He who most entirely agrees with God, he is the most holy man.

(b) A holy man will *endeavor to shun every known sin, and to keep every known commandment.* He will have a decided bent of mind toward God, a hearty desire to do His will, a greater fear of displeasing Him than of displeasing the world, and a love to all His ways. He will feel what Paul felt when he said, "I delight in the law of God after the inward man" (Rom. 7:22), and what David felt when he said, "I esteem *all* thy precepts concerning all things to be right, and I hate *every* false way" (Ps. 119:28).

(c) A holy man will *strive to be like our Lord Jesus Christ.* He will not only live the life of faith in Him, and draw from Him all his daily peace and strength, but he will also labor to have the mind that was in Him, and to be "conformed to his image" (Rom. 8:29). It will be his aim to bear with and forgive others, even as Christ forgave us; to be unselfish, even as Christ pleased not Himself; to walk in love, even as Christ loved us; to be lowly-minded and humble, even as Christ made Himself of no reputation and humbled Himself. He will remember that Christ was a faithful witness for the truth, that He came not to do His own will, that it was His meat and drink to do His Father's will, that He would continually deny Himself in order to minister to others, that He was meek and patient under undeserved insults, that He thought more of godly poor men than of kings, that He was full of love and compassion to sinners, that He was bold and uncompromising in denouncing sin, that He sought not the praise of men, when He might have had it, that He went about doing good, that He was separate from worldly people, that He continued instant in prayer, that He would not let even His nearest relations stand in His way when God's work was to be done. These things a holy man will try to remember. By them he will endeavor to shape his course in life. He will lay to heart the saying of John, "He that saith he abideth in Christ ought himself also so to walk, even as he walked" (I John 2:6); and the saying of Peter, that "Christ suffered for us, leaving us an example that ye should follow his steps" (I Peter 2:21). Happy is he who has learned to make Christ his "all," both for salvation and example! Much time would be saved, and much sin prevented, if men would oftener ask themselves the question, "What would Christ have said and done, if He were in my place?"

(d) A holy man will follow after *meekness,* longsuffering, gentleness, patience, kind tempers, government of his tongue. He will bear much, forbear much, overlook much, and be slow to talk of standing on his rights. We see a bright example of this in the behavior of David when Shimei cursed him, and of Moses when Aaron and Miriam spake against him (II Sam. 16:10; Num. 12:3).

(e) A holy man will follow after *temperance and self-denial.* He will labor to mortify the desires of his body, to crucify his flesh with his affections and lusts, to curb his passions, to restrain his carnal inclinations, lest at any time they break loose. Oh, what a word is that of the Lord Jesus to the apostles, "Take heed to yourselves, lest at any time your hearts be overcharged with surfeiting and drunkenness, and cares of this life'' (Luke 21:34); and that of the apostle Paul, ''I keep under my body, and bring it into subjection, lest that by any means when I have preached to others, I myself should be a castaway'' (I Cor. 9:27).

(f) A holy man will follow after *charity and brotherly kindness*. He will endeavor to observe the golden rule of doing as he would have men to do him, and speaking as he would have men speak to him. He will be full of affection towards his brethren—towards their bodies, their property, their characters, their feelings, their souls. ''He that loveth another,'' says Paul, ''hath fulfilled the law'' (Rom. 13:8). He will abhor all lying, slandering, backbiting, cheating, dishonesty, and unfair dealing, even in the least things. The shekel and cubit of the sanctuary were larger than those in common use. He will strive to adorn his religion by all his outward demeanor, and to make it lovely and beautiful in the eyes of all around him. Alas, what condemning words are the thirteenth chapter of I Corinthians, and the Sermon on the Mount, when laid alongside the conduct of many professing Christians!

(g) A holy man will follow after a spirit of *mercy and benevolence towards others*. He will not stand all the day idle. He will not be content with doing no harm—he will try to do good. He will strive to be useful in his day and generation, and to lessen the spiritual wants and misery around him, as far as he can. Such was Dorcas, ''full of good works and almsdeeds, which she did'' —not merely purposed and talked about, *but did*. Such was Paul: ''I will very gladly spend and be spent for you,'' he says, ''though the more abundantly I love you the less I be loved'' (Acts 9:36; II Cor. 12:15).

(h) A holy man will follow after *purity of heart*. He will dread all filthiness and uncleanness of spirit, and

seek to avoid all things that might draw him into it. He knows his own heart is like tinder, and will diligently keep clear of the sparks of temptation. Who shall dare to talk of strength when David can fall? There is many a hint to be gleaned from the ceremonial law. Under it the man who only *touched* a bone, or a dead body, or a grave, or a diseased person, became at once unclean in the sight of God. And these things were emblems and figures. Few Christians are ever too watchful and too particular about this point.

(i) A holy man will follow after *the fear of God*. I do not mean the fear of a slave, who only works because he is afraid of punishment, and would be idle if he did not dread discovery. I mean rather the fear of a child, who wishes to live and move as if he was always before his father's face, because he loves him. What a noble example Nehemiah gives us of this! When he became governor at Jerusalem he might have been chargeable to the Jews, and required of them money for his support. The former governors had done so. There was none to blame him if he did. But he says, "So did not I, because of the fear of God" (Neh. 5:15).

(j) A holy man will follow after *humility*. He will desire, in lowliness of mind, to esteem all others better than himself. He will see more evil in his own heart than in any other in the world. He will understand something of Abraham's feeling, when he says, "I am dust and ashes"; and Jacob's, when he says, "I am less than the least of all thy mercies"; and Job's, when he says, "I am vile"; and Paul's, when he says, "I am chief of sinners." Holy Bradford, that faithful martyr of Christ, would sometimes finish his letters with these words, "A most miserable sinner, John Bradford." Good old Mr. Grimshaw's last words, when he lay on his deathbed, were these, "Here goes an unprofitable servant."

(k) A holy man will follow after *faithfulness in all the duties and relations in life.* He will try, not merely to fill his place as well as others who take no thought for their souls, but even better, because he has higher motives, and more help than they. Those words of Paul should never be forgotten: "Whatever ye do, do it heartily, as unto the Lord"; "Not slothful in business, fervent in spirit, serving the Lord" (Col. 3:23; Rom. 12:11). Holy persons should aim at doing everything well, and should be ashamed of allowing themselves to do anything ill if they can help it. Like Daniel, they should seek to give no "occasion" against themselves, except "concerning the law of their God" (Dan. 6:5). They should strive to be good husbands and good wives, good parents and good children, good masters and good servants, good neighbors, good friends, good subjects, good in private and good in public, good in the place of business and good by their firesides. Holiness is worth little indeed, if it does not bear this kind of fruit. The Lord Jesus puts a searching question to His people, when He says, "What do ye more than others?" (Matt. 5:47).

(l) Last, but not least, a holy man will follow after *spiritual mindedness.* He will endeavor to set his affections entirely on things above, and to hold things on earth with a very loose hand. He will not neglect the business of the life that now is; but the first place in his mind and thoughts will be given to the life to come. He will aim to live like one whose treasure is in heaven, and to pass through this world like a stranger and pilgrim traveling to his home. To commune with God in prayer, in the Bible, and in the assembly of His people—these things will be the holy man's chief enjoyments. He will value every thing and place and company, just in proportion as it draws him nearer to God. He will enter into something of David's feeling, when he says, "My soul

followeth hard after thee''; ''Thou art my portion'' (Ps. 63:8; 119:57).

Such is the outline of holiness which I venture to sketch out. Such is the character which those who are called ''holy'' *follow after*. Such are the main features of a holy man.

But here let me say, I trust no man will misunderstand me. I am not without fear that my meaning will be mistaken, and the description I have given of holiness will discourage some tender conscience. I would not willingly make one righteous heart sad, or throw a stumbling block in any believer's way.

I do not say for a moment that holiness shuts out the presence of *indwelling* sin. No, far from it. It is the greatest misery of a holy man that he carries about with him a ''body of death''; that often when he would do good ''evil is present with him''; that the old man is clogging all his movements, and, as it were, trying to draw him back at every step he takes (Rom. 7:21). But it is the excellence of a holy man that he is not at peace with indwelling sin, as others are. He hates it, mourns over it, and longs to be free from its company. The work of sanctification within him is like the wall of Jerusalem —the building goes forward ''even in troublous times'' (Dan. 9:25).

Neither do I say that holiness comes to ripeness and perfection all at once, or that these graces I have touched on must be found in full bloom and vigor before you can call a man holy. No, far from it. Sanctification is always a *progressive work*. Some men's graces are in the blade, some in the ear, and some are like full corn in the ear. All must have a beginning. We must never despise ''the day of small things.'' And sanctification in the very best is an *imperfect work*. The history of the brightest saints that ever lived will contain many a ''but,'' and ''howbe-

it,'' and ''notwithstanding,'' before you reach the end.
The gold will never be without some dross, the light will
never shine without some clouds, until we reach the
heavenly Jerusalem. The sun himself has spots upon his
face. The holiest men have many a blemish and defect
when weighed in the balance of the sanctuary. Their life
is a continual warfare with sin, the world, and the devil;
and sometimes you will see them not overcoming, but
overcome. The flesh is ever lusting against the spirit,
and the spirit against the flesh, and ''in many things
they offend all'' (Gal. 5:17; James 3:2).

But still, for all this, I am sure that to have such a
character as I have faintly drawn, is the heart's desire and
prayer of all true Christians. They press towards it, if
they do not reach it. They may not attain to it, but they
always aim at it. It is what they strive and labor to be, if
it is not what they are.

And this I do boldly and confidently say, that true
holiness is a great *reality*. It is something in a man that
can be seen, and known, and marked, and felt by all
around him. It is light: if it exists, it will show itself. It is
salt: if it exists, its savor will be perceived. It is a precious
ointment: if it exists, its presence cannot be hid.

I am sure we should all be ready to make allowance
for much backsliding, for much occasional deadness in
professing Christians. I know a road may lead from one
point to another, and yet have many a winding and
turn; and a man may be truly holy, and yet be drawn
aside by many an infirmity. Gold is not the less gold because mingled with alloy, nor light the less light because
faint and dim, nor grace the less grace because young
and weak. But after every allowance, I cannot see how
any man deserves to be called ''holy,'' who willfully
allows himself in sins, and is not humbled and ashamed
because of them. I dare not call any one ''holy'' who

makes a habit of willfully neglecting known duties, and willfully doing what he knows God has commanded him not to do. Well says Owen, "I do not understand how a man can be a true believer unto whom sin is not the greatest burden, sorrow, and trouble."

Such are the leading characteristics of practical holiness. Let us examine ourselves and see whether we are acquainted with it. Let us prove our own selves.

II. Let me try, in the next place, *to show some reasons why practical holiness is so important.*

Can holiness save us? Can holiness put away sin, cover iniquities, make satisfaction for transgressions, pay our debt to God? No, not a whit. God forbid that I should ever say so. Holiness can do none of these things. The brightest saints are all "unprofitable servants." Our purest works are no better than filthy rags, when tried by the light of God's holy law. The white robe which Jesus offers, and faith puts on, must be our only righteousness, the name of Christ our only confidence, the Lamb's book of life our only title to heaven. With all our holiness we are no better than *sinners.* Our best things are stained and tainted with imperfection. They are all more or less incomplete, wrong in the motive or defective in the performance. By the deeds of the law shall no child of Adam ever be justified. "By grace are ye saved through faith; and that not of yourselves: it is the gift of God: not of works, lest any man should boast" (Eph. 2:8, 9).

Why then is holiness so important? Why does the apostle say, "Without it no man shall see the Lord"? Let me set out in order a few reasons.

(a) For one thing, we must be holy, because *the voice of God in Scripture plainly commands it.* The Lord Jesus says to His people, "Except your righteousness shall ex-

ceed the righteousness of the scribes and Pharisees, ye shall in no case enter into the kingdom of heaven" (Matt. 5:20). "Be ye perfect, even as your Father which is in heaven is perfect" (Matt. 5:48). Paul tells the Thessalonians, "This is the will of God, even your sanctification" (I Thess. 4:3). And Peter says, "As he which hath called you is holy, so be ye holy in all manner of conversation; because it is written, Be ye holy, for I am holy" (I Peter 1:15, 16). "In this," says Leighton, "law and Gospel agree."

(b) We must be holy, because this is one grand *end and purpose for which Christ came into the world*. Paul writes to the Corinthians, "He died for all, that they which live should not henceforth live unto themselves, but unto him which died for them, and rose again" (II Cor. 5:15). And to the Ephesians, "Christ loved the church, and gave himself for it, that he might sanctify and cleanse it" (Eph. 5:25, 26). And to Titus, "He gave himself for us, that he might redeem us from all iniquity, and purify unto himself a peculiar people, zealous of good works" (Titus 2:14). In short, to talk of men being saved from the guilt of sin, without being at the same time saved from its dominion in their hearts, is to contradict the witness of all Scripture. Are believers said to be elect? It is "through sanctification of the Spirit." Are they predestinated? It is "to be conformed to the image of God's Son." Are they chosen? It is "that they may be holy." Are they called? It is "with a holy calling." Are they afflicted? It is that they may be "partakers of holiness." Jesus is a complete Savior. He does not merely take away the guilt of a believer's sin, He does more—He breaks its power (I Peter 1:2; Rom. 8:29; Eph. 1:4; Heb. 12:10).

(c) We must be holy, because this is the *only sound evidence that we have a saving faith in our Lord Jesus*

Christ. The twelfth article of our church says truly, that "Although good works cannot put away our sins, and endure the severity of God's judgment, yet are they pleasing and acceptable to God in Christ, and do spring out necessarily of a true and lively faith; insomuch that by them a lively faith may be as evidently known as a tree discerned by its fruits." James warns us there is such a thing as a dead faith—a faith which goes no further than the profession of the lips, and has no influence on a man's character (James 2:17). True saving faith is a very different kind of thing. True faith will always show itself by its fruits—it will sanctify, it will work by love, it will overcome the world, it will purify the heart. I know that people are fond of talking about deathbed evidences. They will rest on words spoken in the hours of fear, and pain, and weakness, as if they might take comfort in them about the friends they lose. But I am afraid in ninety-nine cases out of a hundred such evidences are not to be depended on. I suspect that, with rare exceptions, men die just as they have lived. The only safe evidence that we are one with Christ, and Christ in us, is holy life. They that live unto the Lord are generally the only people who die in the Lord. If we would die the death of the righteous, let us not rest in slothful desires only; let us seek to live His life. It is a true saying of Traill's, "That man's state is naught, and his faith unsound, that finds not his hopes of glory purifying to his heart and life."

   (d) We must be holy, because this is the *only proof that we love the Lord Jesus Christ in sincerity.* This is a point on which He has spoken most plainly, in the fourteenth and fifteenth chapters of John. "If ye love me, keep my commandments"; "He that hath my commandments and keepeth them, he it is that loveth me"; "If a man love me, he will keep my words"; "Ye are my

friends if ye do whatsoever I command you" (John 14:15, 21, 23; 15:14). Plainer words than these it would be difficult to find, and woe to those who neglect them! Surely that man must be in an unhealthy state of soul who can think of all that Jesus suffered, and yet cling to those sins for which that suffering was undergone. It was sin that wove the crown of thorns; it was sin that pierced our Lord's hands, and feet, and side; it was sin that brought Him to Gethsemane and Calvary, to the cross, and to the grave. Cold must our hearts be if we do not hate sin and labor to get rid of it, though we may have to cut off the right hand and pluck out the right eye in doing it.

(e) We must be holy, because this is the *only sound evidence that we are true children of God*. Children in this world are generally like their parents. Some, doubtless, are more so, and some less, but it is seldom indeed that you cannot trace a kind of family likeness. And it is much the same with the children of God. The Lord Jesus says, "If ye were Abraham's children, ye would do the works of Abraham"; "If God were your Father, ye would love me" (John 8:39, 42). If men have no likeness to the Father in heaven, it is vain to talk of their being His "sons." If we know nothing of holiness we may flatter ourselves as we please, but we have not got the Holy Spirit dwelling in us. We are dead, and must be brought to life again; we are lost, and must be found. "As many as are led by the Spirit of God, they," and they only, "are the sons of God" (Rom. 8:14). We must show by our lives the family we belong to. We must let men see by our good conversation that we are indeed the children of the Holy One, or our sonship is but an empty name. "Say not," says Gurnall, "that thou hast royal blood in thy veins, and art born of God, except thou canst prove thy pedigree by daring to be holy."

(f) We must be holy, because this is the *most likely way to do good to others*. We cannot live to ourselves only in this world. Our lives will always be doing either good or harm to those who see them. They are a silent sermon which all can read. It is sad indeed when they are a sermon for the devil's cause, and not for God's. I believe that far more is done for Christ's kingdom by the holy living of believers than we are at all aware of. There is a reality about such living which makes men feel, and obliges them to think. It carries a weight and influence with it which nothing else can give. It makes religion beautiful, and draws men to consider it, like a lighthouse seen afar off. The day of judgment will prove that many besides husbands have been won *"without the word"* by a holy life (I Peter 3:1). You may talk to persons about the doctrines of the gospel, and few will listen, and still fewer understand. But your life is an argument that none can escape. There is a meaning about holiness which not even the most unlearned can help taking in. They may not understand justification, but they can understand charity.

I believe there is far more harm done by unholy and inconsistent Christians than we are at all aware of. Such men are among Satan's best allies. They pull down by their lives what ministers build with their lips. They cause the chariot wheels of the gospel to drive heavily. They supply the children of this world with a never-ending excuse for remaining as they are. "I cannot see the use of so much religion," said an irreligious tradesman not long ago. "I observe that some of my customers are always talking about the gospel, and faith, and election, and the blessed promises, and so forth; and yet these very people think nothing of cheating me of pence and halfpence, when they have an opportunity. Now, if religious persons can do such things, I do not see what good there is in religion." I grieve to be obliged to write such things, but I fear that Christ's name is too often blasphemed because of the lives of Christians. Let us take heed lest the blood of souls should be required at our hands. From murder of souls by inconsistency and loose walking, good Lord, deliver us! Oh, for the sake of others, if for no other reason, let us strive to be holy!

(g) We must be holy, *because our present comfort depends much upon it*. We cannot be too often reminded of this. We are sadly apt to forget that there is a close connection between sin and sorrow, holiness and happiness, sanctification and consolation. God has so wisely ordered it, that our well-being and our well-doing are linked together. He has mercifully provided that even in this world it shall be man's *interest* to be holy. Our justification is not by works—our calling and election are not according to our works—but it is vain for any one to suppose that he will have a lively *sense* of his justification, or an *assurance* of his calling, so long as he neglects good works, or does not strive to live a holy life. "Hereby we do know that we know him, if we keep his commandments"; "Hereby we know that we are of the truth, and shall assure our hearts" (I John 2:3; 3:19). A believer may as soon expect to feel the sun's rays upon a dark and cloudy day, as to feel strong consolation in Christ while he does not follow Him fully. When the disciples forsook the Lord and fled, they escaped danger, but they were miserable and sad. When, shortly after, they confessed Him boldly before men, they were cast into prison and beaten; but we are told "they rejoiced that they were counted worthy to suffer shame for his name" (Acts 5:41). Oh, for our own sakes, if there were no other reason, let us strive to be holy! He that follows Jesus most fully will always follow Him most comfortably.

(h) Lastly, we must be holy, *because without holiness on earth we shall never be prepared to enjoy heaven.* Heaven is a holy place. The Lord of heaven is a holy being. The angels are holy creatures. Holiness is written on everything in heaven. The Book of Revelation says expressly, "There shall in no wise enter into it anything that defileth, neither whatsoever worketh abomination, or maketh a lie" (Rev. 21:27).

I appeal solemnly to every one who reads these pages, How shall we ever be at home and happy in heaven, if we die unholy? Death works no change. The grave makes no alteration. Each will rise again with the same character in which he breathed his last. Where will our place be if we are strangers to holiness now?

Suppose for a moment that you were allowed to enter heaven without holiness. What would you do? What possible enjoyment could you feel there? To which of all the saints would you join yourself, and by whose side would you sit down? Their pleasures are not your pleasures, their tastes not your tastes, their character not your character. How could you possibly be happy, if you had not been holy on earth?

Now perhaps you love the company of the light and the careless, the worldly-minded and the covetous, the reveler and the pleasure-seeker, the ungodly and the profane. There will be none such in heaven.

Now perhaps you think the saints of God too strict and particular, and serious. You rather avoid them. You have no delight in their society. There will be no other company in heaven.

Now perhaps you think praying, and Scripture reading, and hymn singing, dull, and melancholy, and stupid work—a thing to be tolerated now and then, but not enjoyed. You reckon the Sabbath a burden and a weariness; you could not possibly spend more than a small part of it in worshiping God. But remember, heaven is a never-ending Sabbath. The inhabitants thereof rest not day or night, singing, "Holy, holy, holy, Lord God Almighty," and singing the praise of the Lamb. How could an unholy man find pleasure in occupation such as this?

Think you that such a one would delight to meet David, and Paul, and John, after a life spent in doing the very things they spoke against? Would he take sweet counsel with them, and find that he and they had much in common? Think you, above all, that he would rejoice to meet Jesus, the crucified one, face to face, after cleaving to the sins for which He died, after loving His enemies and despising His friends? Would he stand before Him with confidence, and join in the cry, "This is our God; we have waited for him, we will be glad and rejoice in his salvation"? (Isa. 25:9). Think you not rather that the tongue of an unholy man would cleave to the roof of his mouth with shame, and his only desire would be to be cast out? He would feel a stranger in a land he knew not, a black sheep amidst Christ's holy flock. The voice of cherubim and seraphim, the song of angels and archangels, and all the company of heaven, would be a language he could not understand. The very air would seem an air he could not breathe.

I know not what others may think, but to me it does seem clear that heaven would be a miserable place to an unholy man. It cannot be otherwise. People may say, in a vague way, "they hope to go to heaven"; but they do not consider what they say. There must be a certain "meetness for the inheritance of the saints in light." Our hearts must be somewhat in tune. To reach the holiday of glory, we must pass through the training school of grace. We must be heavenly-minded, and have heavenly tastes, in the life that now is, or else we shall never find ourselves in heaven, in the life to come.

And now, before I go any further, let me say a few words, by way of application.

(1) For one thing, let me ask every one who may read these pages, *Are you holy?* Listen, I pray you, to the question I put to you this day. Do you know anything of the holiness of which I have been speaking?

I do not ask whether you attend your church regularly, whether you have been baptized, and received the Lord's Supper, whether you have the name of Christian. I ask something more than all this: *Are you holy, or are you not?*

I do not ask whether you approve of holiness in others, whether you like to read the lives of holy people, and to talk of holy things, and to have on your table holy books, whether you mean to be holy, and hope you will be holy some day. I ask something further: *Are you yourself holy this very day, or are you not?*

And why do I ask so straitly, and press the question so strongly? I do it because the Scripture says, "Without holiness no man shall see the Lord." It is written, it is not my fancy; it is the Bible, not my private opinion; it is the Word of God, not of man—*"Without holiness no man shall see the Lord"* (Heb. 12:14).

Alas, what searching, sifting words are these! What thoughts come across my mind, as I write them down! I look at the world, and see the greater part of it lying in wickedness. I look at professing Christians, and see the vast majority having nothing of Christianity but the name. I turn to the Bible, and I hear the Spirit saying, "Without holiness no man shall see the Lord."

Surely it is a text that ought to make us consider our ways, and search our hearts. Surely it should raise within us solemn thoughts, and send us to prayer.

You may try to put me off by saying, "You feel much, and think much about these things, far more than many suppose." I answer, "This is not the point. The poor lost souls in hell do as much as this. The great question is not what you *think*, and what you *feel*, but what you DO."

You may say, "It was never meant that all Christians should be holy, and that holiness, such as I have described, is only for great saints, and people of uncommon gifts." I answer, "I cannot see that in Scripture. I read that *every man* who hath hope in Christ purifieth himself" (I John 3:3). "Without holiness *no man* shall see the Lord."

You may say, "It is impossible to be so holy and to do our duty in this life at the same time; the thing cannot be done." I answer, "You are mistaken. It *can* be done. With Christ on your side nothing is impossible. It *has* been done by many. David, and Obadiah, and Daniel, and the servants of Nero's household, are all examples that go to prove it."

You may say, "If you were so holy you would be unlike other people." I answer, "I know it well. It is just what you ought to be. Christ's true servants always were unlike the world around them—a separate nation, a peculiar people—and you must be so too, if you would be saved!"

You may say, "At this rate very few will be saved." I answer, "I know it. It is precisely what we are told in the Sermon on the Mount." The Lord Jesus said so 1800 years ago. "Strait is the gate, and narrow is the way, that leadeth unto life, and few there be that find it" (Matt. 7:14). Few will be saved, because few will take the trouble to seek salvation. Men will not deny themselves the pleasures of sin and their own way for a little season. They turn their backs on an "inheritance incorruptible, undefiled, and that fadeth not away." "Ye will not come unto me," says Jesus, "that ye might have life."

You may say, "These are hard sayings; the way is very narrow." I answer, "I know it. So says the Sermon on the Mount." The Lord Jesus said so 1800 years ago. He always said that men must take up the cross daily, and that they must be ready to cut off hand or foot, if they would be His disciples. It is in religion as it is in other things: "There are no gains without pains." That which costs nothing is worth nothing.

Whatever we may think fit to say, we must be holy, if we would see the Lord. Where is our Christianity if we are not? We must not merely have a Christian name, and Christian knowledge, we must have a Christian *character* also. We must be saints on earth, if ever we mean to be saints in heaven. God has said it, and He will not go back: "Without holiness no man shall see the Lord." "The Pope's calendar," says Jenkyn, "only makes saints of the *dead*, but Scripture requires sanctity in the *living*." "Let not men deceive themselves," says Owen; "sanctification is a qualification indispensably necessary unto those who will be under the conduct of the Lord Christ unto salvation. He leads none to heaven but whom He sanctifies on the earth. This living Head will not admit of dead members."

Surely we need not wonder that Scripture says "Ye must be born again" (John 3:7). Surely it is clear as noon-day that many professing Christians need a complete change—new hearts, new natures—if ever they are to be saved. Old things must pass away; they must become new creatures. "Without holiness no man," be he who he may, "no man shall see the Lord."

(2) Let me, for another thing, speak a little to believers. I ask you this question, "*Do you think you feel the importance of holiness as much as you should?*"

I own I fear the temper of the times about this subject. I doubt exceedingly whether it holds that place which it deserves in the thoughts and attention of some of the Lord's people. I would humbly suggest that we are apt to overlook the doctrine of growth in grace, and that we do not sufficiently consider how very far a person may go in a profession of religion, and yet have no grace, and be dead in God's sight after all. I believe that Judas Iscariot seemed very like the other apostles. When the Lord warned them that one would betray Him, no one said, "Is it Judas?" We had better think more about the churches of Sardis and Laodicea than we do.

I have no desire to make an idol of holiness. I do not wish to dethrone Christ, and put holiness in His place. But I must candidly say, I wish sanctification was more thought of in this day than it seems to be, and I therefore take occasion to press the subject on all believers into whose hands these pages fall. I fear it is sometimes forgotten that God has married together justification and sanctification. They are distinct and different things, beyond question, but one is never found without the other. All justified people are sanctified, and all sanctified are justified. What God has joined together let no man dare to put asunder. Tell me not of your justification, unless you have also some marks of sanctification. Boast not of Christ's work *for you*, unless you can show us the Spirit's work *in you*. Think not that Christ and the Spirit can ever be divided. I doubt not that many believers know these things, but I think it good for us to be put in remembrance of them. Let us prove that we know them by our lives. Let us try to keep in view this text more continually: "Follow holiness, without which no man shall see the Lord."

I must frankly say, I wish there was not such an excessive *sensitiveness* on the subject of holiness as I sometimes perceive in the minds of believers. A man might really think it was a dangerous subject to handle, so cautiously is it touched! Yet surely when we have exalted Christ as "the way, the truth, and the life," we cannot err in speaking strongly about what should be the character of His people. Well says Rutherford, "The way that crieth down duties and sanctification, is not the way of grace. Believing and doing are blood-friends."

I would say it with all reverence, but say it I must—I sometimes fear if Christ were on earth now, there are not a few who would think His preaching *legal*; and if Paul were writing his epistles, there are those who would think he had better not write the latter part of most of them as he did. But let us remember that the Lord Jesus *did* speak the Sermon on the Mount, and that the Epistle to the Ephesians contains six chapters and not four. I grieve to feel obliged to speak in this way, but I am sure there is a cause.

That great divine, John Owen, the Dean of Christ Church, used to say, more than two hundred years ago, that there were people whose whole religion seemed to consist in going about complaining of their own corruptions, and telling everyone that they could do nothing of themselves. I am afraid that after two centuries the same thing might be said with truth of some of Christ's professing people in this day. I know there are texts in Scripture which warrant such complaints. I do not object to them when they come from men who walk in the steps of the apostle Paul, and fight a good fight, as he did, against sin, the devil, and the world. But I never like such complaints when I see ground for suspecting, as I often do, that they are only a cloak to cover spiritual laziness, and an excuse for spiritual sloth. If we say with Paul, "O wretched man that I am," let us also be able to say with him, "I press toward the mark." Let us not quote his example in one thing, while we do not follow him in another (Rom. 7:24; Phil. 3:14).

I do not set up myself to be better than other people, and if anyone asks, "What are you, that you write in this way?" I answer, "I am a very poor creature indeed." But I say that I cannot read the Bible without desiring to see many believers more spiritual, more holy, more single-eyed, more heavenly-minded, more whole-hearted than they are in the nineteenth century. I want to see among believers more of a pilgrim spirit, a more decided separation from the world, a conversation more evidently in heaven, a closer walk with God—and therefore I have written as I have.

Is it not true that we need a higher standard of personal holiness in this day? Where is our patience? Where is our zeal? Where is our love? Where are our works? Where is the power of religion to be seen, as it was in time gone by? Where is that unmistakable tone which used to distinguish the saints of old, and shake the world? Verily our silver has become dross, our wine mixed with water, and our salt has very little savor. We are all more than half asleep. The night is far spent, and the day is at hand. Let us awake, and sleep no more. Let us open our eyes more widely than we have done hitherto. "Let us lay aside every weight, and the sin that doth so easily beset us." "Let us cleanse ourselves from all filthiness of flesh and spirit, and perfect holiness in the fear of God" (Heb. 12:1; II Cor. 7:1). "Did Christ die," says Owen, "and shall sin live? Was He crucified in the world, and shall our affections to the world be quick and lively? Oh, where is the spirit of him, who by the cross of Christ was crucified to the world, and the world to him?"

III. Let me, in the last place, offer a *word of advice to all who desire to be holy.*

Would you be holy? Would you become a new creature? Then you must *begin with Christ.* You will do just nothing at all, and make no progress till you feel your sin and weakness, and flee to Him. He is the root and beginning of all holiness, and the way to be holy is to come to Him by faith and be joined to Him. Christ is not wisdom and righteousness only to His people, but sanctification also. Men sometimes try to make themselves holy first of all, and sad work they make of it. They toil and labor, and turn over many new leaves, and make many changes; and yet, like the woman with the issue of blood, before she came to Christ, they feel "nothing bettered, but rather worse" (Mark 5:26). They run in vain, and labor in vain; and little wonder, for they are beginning at the wrong end. They are building up a wall of sand; their work runs down as fast as they throw it up. They are baling water out of a leaky vessel: the leak gains on them, not they on the leak. Other foundation of "holiness" can no man lay than that which Paul laid, even Christ Jesus. "Without Christ we can do nothing" (John 15:5). It is a strong but true saying of Traill's, "Wisdom out of Christ is damning folly, righteousness out of Christ is guilt and condemnation, sanctification out of Christ is filth and sin, redemption out of Christ is bondage and slavery."

Do you want to attain holiness? Do you feel this day a real hearty desire to be holy? Would you be a partaker of the divine nature? Then *go to Christ.* Wait for nothing. Wait for nobody. Linger not. Think not to make yourself ready. Go and say to Him, in the words of that beautiful hymn—

> Nothing in my hand I bring,
> Simply to Thy cross I cling;
> Naked, flee to Thee for dress;
> Helpless, look to Thee for grace.

There is not a brick nor a stone laid in the work of our sanctification till we go to Christ. Holiness is His special gift to His believing people. Holiness is the work He carries on in their hearts, by the Spirit whom He puts within them. He is appointed a "Prince and a Saviour, to give repentance" as well as remission of sins. "To as many as receive him, he gives power to become sons of God" (Acts 5:31; John 1:12, 13). Holiness comes not of blood—parents cannot give it to their children; nor yet of the will of the flesh—man cannot produce it in himself; nor yet of the will of man—ministers cannot give it you by baptism. Holiness comes from Christ. It is the result of vital union with Him. It is the fruit of being a living branch of the true vine. Go then to Christ and say, "Lord, not only save me from the guilt of sin, but send the Spirit, whom thou didst promise, and save me from its power. Make me holy. Teach me to do thy will."

Would you continue holy? Then *abide in Christ*. He says Himself, "Abide in me and I in you. . . . He that abideth in me and I in him, the same beareth much fruit" (John 15:4, 5). It pleased the Father that in Him should all fullness dwell—a full supply for all a believer's wants. He is the physician to whom you must daily go, if you would keep well. He is the manna which you must daily eat, and the rock of which you must daily drink. His arm is the arm on which you must daily lean, as you come up out of the wilderness of this world. You must not only be rooted, you must also be *built up* in Him. Paul was a man of God indeed, a holy man, a growing, thriving Christian. And what was the secret of it all? He was one to whom Christ was "all in all." He was ever "looking unto Jesus." "I can do all things," he says, "through Christ which strengtheneth me." "I live, yet not I, but Christ liveth in me. The life that I now live, I live by the faith of the Son of God." Let us go and do likewise (Heb. 12:2; Phil. 4:13; Gal. 2:20).

May all who read these pages know these things by experience, and not by hearsay only! May we all feel the importance of holiness, far more than we have ever done yet! May our years be *holy years* with our souls, and then they will be happy ones! Whether we live, may we live unto the Lord; or whether we die, may we die unto the Lord; or if He comes for us, may we be found in peace, without spot, and blameless!

3
Regeneration

"Verily, verily, I say unto thee, Except a man be
born again, he cannot see the kingdom of
God."—John 3:3

If the Bible be false, as some proud men have
dared to say, there is no occasion for keeping one day in
the week holy, there is no use in honoring church and
making a profession of religion; we are no better than
the beasts that perish, and the best thing a man can do is
to eat and drink and live as he pleases. If the Bible be
only half truth, as some unhappy people strive to make
out, there is no certainty about our everlasting souls:
Christianity is all doubt and dimness and guesswork, we
can never know what we are to believe as necessary to
salvation, we can never be sure that we have got hold of
the words of eternal life. Give up your Bible, and you
have not a square inch of certainty and confidence to
stand on: you may think and you may fancy and you
may have your own opinion, but you cannot show me
any satisfactory proof or authority that you are right; you
are building merely on your own judgment; you have
put out your own eyes, as it were, and, like one in the
dark, you do not really know where you are going.

But if, beloved, the Bible be indeed the Word of God Himself and altogether true, and that it is so can be proved by witnesses without number; if the Bible be indeed true and our only guide to heaven, and this I trust you are all ready to allow, it surely must be the duty of every wise and thinking man to lay to heart each doctrine which it contains, and while he adds nothing to it, to be careful that he takes nothing from it.

Now, I say that on the face of the Bible, when fairly read, there stands out this grand doctrine, that we must each of us between the cradle and grave go through a spiritual change, a change of heart, or in other words be born again; and in the text you have heard read the Lord Jesus declares positively, without it no man shall see the kingdom of God.

Sinner, man or woman, mark that! No salvation without this new birth! Christ hath done everything for thee; He paid the price of our redemption, lived for us, died for us, rose again for us; but all shall avail us nothing, if there be not this work in us: *we must be born again*.

Now, beloved, I desire to speak to you freely and plainly about this new birth, in two or three sermons, as a thing absolutely necessary to salvation; and today, at least, I shall try to show you from my text two things: *first*, the reason why we must all be born again, and *secondly*, what the expression to be born again means; and the Lord grant that the subject to which I am going to call your attention for two or three Sunday mornings may not be listened to and soon forgotten, as a light and indifferent matter—but carried home and thought over, and blessed to the conversion of many souls!

I. Why, then, is this change of heart so necessary? The answer is short and simple. Because of the natural sinfulness of every man's disposition. We are not born into the world with spotless, innocent minds, but corrupt and wicked, and with a will to the thing which is evil as soon as we have the power; and the scriptural account is true to the letter—we are all conceived in sin and shapen in iniquity. I need not stop now to tell you how all this came to pass; I need only remind you that in the beginning it was not so. Our first parents, Adam and Eve, were created holy, harmless, undefiled, without spot or stain or blemish about them; and when God rested from His labor on the seventh day, He pronounced them, like all His other works, to be very good. But, alas for us! Adam, by transgression, fell, and lost his first estate; he forfeited the likeness of God in which he had been made; and hence all we, who are his children, come into being with a defiled and sinful nature. We are fallen, and we must needs be raised; we have about us the marks of the old Adam—Adam the first, earthly and carnal—and we must needs be marked with the marks of the second Adam, the Lord Jesus, which are heavenly and spiritual. Do any of you feel a doubt of this? Consider only what we are by nature.

By nature we do not see Christ's spiritual kingdom upon earth; it is all hid from our eyes. Men may be sharp and knowing in worldly matters, they may be wise in the things of time; but when they come to religion, their understandings seem blind, there is a thick veil over their hearts, and they see nothing as they ought to see.

So long as they are in this natural state it is in vain they are told of God's holiness and God's unchangeable justice, His spiritual law and His judgment to come, their own enormous deficiencies, their own peril of destruction—it matters not; it all falls flat and dull upon their ears; they neither feel it nor care for it nor consider it, and in a few hours they are as though they had never heard it. It is to no purpose, while in this condition, that Christ crucified and His precious atonement are set before us; we can see no form nor beauty nor comeliness about Him; we cannot value what He has done, and, as far as we are concerned, the wisdom and the excellence of the cross, which apostles gloried in, seems all thrown away. And why is this? Our hearts want changing. "The natural man receiveth not the things of the Spirit of God: for they are foolishness unto him: neither can he know them, because they are spiritually discerned" (I Cor. 2:14) This is the true account of all that weariness and lifelessness and carelessness which we so often see in the worshipers of God's house; this is the secret of that awful indifference about spiritual things which prevails so widely both among rich and poor, and makes the gospel appear a sealed book. It comes from the heart. Some always fancy they want learning, some have no time, some have very peculiar difficulties which no one else in the world has; but the truth lies far deeper. They all want new hearts. Once give them new natures, and you would hear no more about learning, or time, or difficulty. Every mountain would be leveled and every valley filled up, that the way of God might be prepared.

But again. By nature we do not love the laws of Christ's spiritual kingdom. We do not openly refuse to obey them, we should be angry with any one who said we had thrown them aside, but we have no love to them and delight in them; it is not our meat and drink to do our Father's will. Oh no! By nature we love our own way and our own inclinations, and that is our only law. We bring forth fruit unto ourselves, but not unto God. Our own pleasure and our own profit take up all our attention, and as for Him who made us and redeemed us, too many do not give Him the very leavings of their time. By nature we do not measure ourselves by God's standard:

Who ever takes the Sermon on the Mount as his rule of
character? Who ever admires the poor in spirit, the
mourners, the meek, the hungerers and thirsters after
righteousness, the merciful, the pure in heart, the
peacemakers, the men who are persecuted for righteousness' sake? These are all people whom the world
despises, they are as nothing by the side of the jovial and
lighthearted, the men who love strong drink and are
held to sing good songs; and yet these are the persons
whom Jesus calls blessed. What natural man judges of
sin as Jesus teaches us to judge? How few look on
drunkenness and fornication as damnable sins! Yet the
Bible says they are. How few consider anger without
cause as bad as murder, and wanton looks as bad as
adultery! Yet Jesus says they are. Where are the men
who strive to love their enemies, who bless those that
hate them, and pray for those who despitefully use
them? Yet this is the rule that Jesus has laid down. And
why is all this? You see there must be something radi-
cally wrong. By nature we do not lay ourselves out to
glorify God with our bodies and spirits, we take no
pleasure in speaking to each other about Him, the concerns of this world have a hundred times more of our
thoughts; and few indeed are the parties where the mention of Christ and heaven would not stop many mouths,
and make nearly all look as if the subject was very uncomfortable. And why is all this? Some talk of bad example having done them harm, and some say they have
had a bad education, but the evil is far more deeply
seated; that which is born of the flesh is flesh, it comes
from the carnal unrenewed mind, and the remedy
wanted is change of nature. A corrupt tree can only
bring forth corrupt fruit; the root of the mischief is the
natural heart.

Once more. By nature we are altogether unfit for
Christ's kingdom in glory. The lives which we are in the

habit of leading, and the practices we are fond of in-
dulging, and the tastes we are always seeking to please,
and the opinions we hold, are all such as prove we have
no natural meetness for the inheritance of the saints in
light. They do not follow after holiness in all their walk
and conversation. Then what place can they occupy in
that blessed abode where there shall enter in nothing
that defileth, nor whatsoever worketh abomination?
How shall they stand in His presence, who chargeth even
His angels with folly, and in whose sight the very
heavens are not pure! They do not take pleasure in the
exercise of prayer and praise on earth; and how could
they enjoy the employments of that glorious habitation,
where they rest not day nor night worshiping and crying,
"Holy, holy, holy, Lord God Almighty, which was, and
is, and is to come" (Rev. 4:8). They do not count it a
privilege to draw nigh to God through Jesus Christ, to
walk with Him, to seek close acquaintance with Him;
and where would be the comfort to them of dwelling
forever in the presence of the Lord God and the Lamb?
They do not strive to walk in the steps of holy men of
old, they do not take example from the faith and patience of the saints; and with what face then would they
join the society of just men made perfect? With what
salutation, after a life spent in pleasing the devil and the
world, would they greet Abraham and David and the
apostles and all that blessed company who have fought
the good fight? Alas, beloved, a natural man in heaven
would be a miserable creature—there would be something in the air he could not breathe, the joys, the affections, the employments would be all wearisome to him,
he would find himself unfitted for the company of the
saints, as a beast is unfitted on earth for the company of
man; he would be carnally minded, they would be spiritually minded, there would be nothing in common. I
know there are vain dreamers who fancy death will work

an alteration, that they may die sinners and rise again saints; but it is all a delusion, there is no work nor device nor knowledge in the grave; if we die spiritual we shall rise spiritual, if we die carnal we shall rise carnal, and if we are to be made fit for heaven our natural hearts must be changed now on earth.

In short, beloved, the plain truth is, that by nature men are all dead in trespasses and sins, aliens from the commonwealth of Israel, strangers to the covenant of promise, having no hope and without God in the world, prisoners in the hand of Satan, in a state of miserable condemnation, spiritually dark, blind, and sleeping; and, worst of all, they neither know nor feel it. The cold corpse in the grave does not feel the worms that crawl over it; the sleeping wretch who has unawares drunk poison does not know that he shall wake no more; and so also the unhappy man who is still unconverted cannot understand that he is in need of anything. But still, every natural man in the sight of God is dead while he liveth; his body, soul, and mind are all turned aside from their proper use, which is to glorify God, and so he is looked upon as dead. And this either is the state of every soul among us at this minute, or else it used to be. There is no middle state; we cannot be halfway, neither dead nor alive; we were dead and have been brought to life, or we are now dead, and the work is yet to be done. Nor yet is this doctrine for publicans and harlots only: it is for all without exception; it touches high and low, rich and poor, learned and unlearned, old and young, gentle and simple; all are by nature sinful and corrupt, and because they are so Jesus tells us solemnly not one shall enter into the heavenly rest without being born again.

Beloved, this sounds strong; it seems a hard saying, perhaps. That is not my affair; I am set to preach Christ's gospel and not my own. Search the Scriptures, and you will see it is true.

II. The second thing for your consideration is the exact signification and force of that peculiar expression "to be born again." It is a change by which we once more recover something of the divine nature, and are renewed after the image of God. It is a complete transforming and altering of all the inner man; and nothing can more fully show its completeness and importance than the strong figure under which Jesus describes it: He calls it a NEW BIRTH. We have all been born once as men, but we must see to it we are born again as true Christians. We have been born once of the seed of Adam; woe to us if we are not born the second time of the seed of God! We have been born of the flesh, we must also be born of the Spirit. We are born earthly, we must also be born incorruptible, for our natural birth is not a whit more necessary to the life of the body than is our spiritual birth necessary to the life of the soul.

To be born again is as it were to enter upon a new existence, to have a new mind and a new heart, new views, new principles, new tastes, new affections, new likings and new dislikings, new fears, new joys, new sorrows, new love to things once hated, new hatred to things once loved, new thoughts of God and ourselves and the world and the life to come and the means whereby that life is attained. And it is indeed a true saying that he who has gone through it is a new man, a new creature, for old things are passed away—behold, he can say, all things are become new! It is not so much that our natural powers and faculties are taken away and destroyed; I would rather say that they receive an utterly new bias and direction. It is not that the old metal is cast aside, but it is melted down and refined and remolded, and has a new stamp impressed upon it, and thus, so to speak, becomes a new coin.

This is no outward change, like that of Herod, who did many things and then stopped, or of Ahab, who humbled himself and went in sackcloth and walked softly; nor is it a change which can neither be seen nor felt. It is not merely a new name and a new notion, but the implanting of a new principle which will surely bear good fruit. It is opening the eyes of the blind and unstopping the ears of the deaf; it is loosing the tongue of the dumb, and giving hands and feet to the maimed and lame—for he that is born again no longer allows his members to be instruments and servants of unrighteousness, but he gives them unto God, and then only are they properly employed.

To be born again is to become a member of a new family by adoption, even the family of God; it is to feel that God is indeed our Father, and that we are made the very sons and daughters of the Almighty; it is to become the citizen of a new state, to cast aside the bondage of Satan and live as free men in the glorious liberty of Christ's kingdom, giving our King the tribute of our best affection, and believing that He will keep us from all evil. To be born again is a spiritual resurrection, a faint likeness indeed of the great change at last, but still a likeness; for the new birth of a man is a passage from death to life; it is a passage from ignorance of God to a full knowledge of Him, from slavish fear to childlike love, from sleepy carelessness about Him to fervent desire to please Him, from lazy indifference about salvation to burning, earnest zeal; it is a passage from strangeness towards God to heartfelt confidence, from a state of enmity to a state of peace, from worldliness to holiness, from an earthly, sensual, man-pleasing state of mind to the single-eyed mind that is in Christ Jesus. And this it is to be born of the Spirit.

Beloved, time will not allow me to go further with this subject today. I have endeavored to show you generally why we must all be born again, and what the new birth means; and on Sunday next, if the Lord will, I purpose to show you the manner and means by which this new birth comes.

It only remains for me now to commend this matter most solemnly to your consciences. Were it a doctrine of only second-rate importance, were it a point a man might leave uncertain and yet be saved, like church government or election, I would not press it on you so strongly; but it is one of the two great pillars of the gospel. On the one hand stands salvation by free grace for Christ's sake; but on the other stands renewal of the carnal heart by the Spirit. We must be changed as well as forgiven; we must be renewed as well as redeemed.

And I commend this to you all the more because of the times you live in. Men swallow down sermons about Christ's willingness and Christ's power to save, and yet continue in their sins: they seem to forget there must be the Spirit's work within us, as well as Christ's work for us—there must be something written on the table of our hearts. The strong man, Satan, must be cast out of our house, and Jesus must take possession; and we must begin to know the saints' character experimentally on earth, or we shall never be numbered with them in heaven. Christ is indeed a full and sufficient title to heaven; but we must have about us some meetness and fitness for that blessed abode.

I will not shrink from telling you that this doctrine cuts every congregation in two; it is the line of separation between the good fish and the bad, the wheat and the tares. There is a natural part in every congregation, and there is a spiritual part; and few indeed are the churches where we should not be constrained to cry, Lord, here are many called, but very few chosen. The kingdom of God is no mere matter of lips and knees and outward service—it must be within a man, seated in the best place of heart; and I will not hesitate to tell you I fear there are many living members of churches who are exceedingly dead Christians.

Examine yourselves, then, I pray you, whether you are born again. Have you good solid reasons for thinking that ye have put off the old man which is corrupt, and put on the new man which is created after God in holiness? Are ye renewed in the spirit of your minds? Are ye bringing forth the fruits of the flesh or the fruits of the Spirit? Are ye carnally minded or heavenly minded? Are your affections with the world or with God? Are ye natural men or are ye spiritual men? Oh, but it were no charity in me to keep back this weighty truth; and it will be no wisdom in you to put off and delay considering it.

Are ye born again? Without it no salvation! It is not written that you may not, or yet that you will have some difficulty, but it is written that you cannot without it see the kingdom of God. Consider with yourselves how fearful it will be to be shut out; to see God's kingdom afar off, like the rich man in the parable, and a great gulf between; how terrible to go down to the pit from under the very pulpit, well satisfied with your own condition, but still not born again. There are truly many roads to perdition, but none so melancholy as that which is traveled on by professing Christians—by men and women who have light and knowledge and warning and means and opportunity and yet go smiling on as if sermons and religion were not meant for them, or as if hell were a bed of roses, or as if God were a liar and would not keep His word.

Are ye born again? I do not want to fill your heads, but to move your hearts; it is not a matter of course that all who go to church shall be saved; churches and ministers are meant to rouse you to self-inquiry, to awaken you to a sense of your condition; and next to that grand question, "Have you taken Christ for your Savior?" there comes the second point, "Are you born again?"

Beloved, if you love life, search and see what is your condition. What though you find no tokens for good: better a thousand times to know it now and live, than to know it too late and die eternally!

Praised be God, it is a doctrine bound round with gracious promises: no heart so hard but the Holy Ghost can move it; many a one could set his seal to that, and tell you that he was darkness, darkness that could be felt, but is now light in the Lord. Many of the Corinthians were bad as the worst among you, but they were washed, they were sanctified, they were justified, in the name of the Lord Jesus and by the Spirit of our God. Many of the Ephesians were as completely dead in sins as any of you, but God quickened them, and raised them up, and created them anew unto good works. Examine yourselves and draw nigh to God with prayer, and He shall draw nigh to you; but if ye ask not, ye shall not have.

As for me, I make my supplication unto God, who can make all things new, that His Spirit may touch your hearts with a deep sense of this truth, for without it my preaching is vain; that there may be a mighty shaking and revival among the dry bones; that you may never rest until you are indeed new men and can say, Verily we *were* dead but we are now alive, we *were* lost but we are now found.

About this new birth—without which no man or woman can be saved! You may remember I began to speak of it last Sunday morning, and I endeavored to establish in your minds two main points, which it may be well to recall to your recollection now. First, then, I showed you the reason why this new birth is so absolutely necessary to salvation: it is because of our sinful hearts, our inbred corruption; we are born from the very first with a disposition towards that which is bad; we have no natural readiness to serve God—it is all against the grain; we have no natural insight into the excellence of Christ's spiritual kingdom, no natural love towards His holy laws or desire to obey them, no natural fitness for heaven; an unrenewed man would be miserable in the company of Jesus and the saints. In short, I said, it is not enough that we are born of the flesh once, natural men; we must needs be born the second time of God and become spiritual men, or else we shall never taste eternal life. I then reminded you of the awful carelessness and indifference and deadness and lukewarmness and coldness and slothfulness about religion which doth so widely prevail; and I observed that people were always ingenious in framing reasons and making excuses for their own particular neglect of God, always supposing they had some special difficulty to contend with, which none else had—business, or poverty, trouble, or family, or want of time, or want of learning, and the like— always fancying if these difficulties were taken out of the way they should be such good Christians; and I then told you to mark that the root of all these difficulties is the natural old heart, and the thing wanted is not leisure and ease and money and learning, but a new heart and a new principle within. Secondly, I went on to set before you the nature and character of this new birth. I showed that it was a change not outward only, but inward—not in name only, but in spirit and in truth—a change so thorough, so searching, so radical, so complete, that he who has gone through it may be called born again, for he is to all intents and purposes a new man: he was darkness, but he is now light; he was blind, but he can now see; he was sleeping, but he is now awake; he was dead, but he now lives; he was earthly minded, but he is now heavenly minded; he was carnal, but he is now spiritual; he was worldly, but he is now godly; he once loved most the things corruptible, he now loves the things incorruptible; he did set his chief affections on that which is mortal, he now sets them on immortality.

Lastly, I pressed upon you all the immense, the surpassing importance of this doctrine, and I do so now again. I urged you, every one, to remember—and I repeat it now—it shall avail us nothing that Christ Jesus has brought in righteousness for us, if there be not also the work of the Holy Ghost within us; that it shall profit us nothing to say we are redeemed, if there is not also good evidence that we have been indeed renewed.

I shall now go on, according to my promise, to set before you the first great cause of this new birth, and the means and the manner in which it comes; and I once more pray God that the subject may not be carelessly put aside, but thought over and made useful to all your souls.

I. This new birth, then, this great spiritual change, whence comes it, and how does it begin? Can any man give it to himself when he pleases? Can any change his own heart? No, the thing is impossible! We can no more quicken and impart life to our souls than we can to our bodies; we can no more rise and become new men in our own strength than wash away sins by our own performances. It is impossible! The natural man is as helpless as

Lazarus was when he lay still and cold and motionless in the tomb. We may remove the stone, as it were, and expose the sad work of death, but we can do no more. There must be a power far mightier than any power of earth in exercise before the natural man can awake and arise and come forth as a new creature. And to do all this is the special office of the Spirit of Christ, the Holy Ghost, whom Jesus promised to send. It is He that quickeneth; it is He that giveth life. The Spirit alone can make the seed we scatter bear fruit; the Spirit alone can lay the first foundation of that holy kingdom we want to see established in your hearts. The Spirit must move over these waste and barren souls before they can become the garden of the Lord; the Spirit must open the darkened windows of our conscience before the true light can shine in upon those chambers within us. And so, he that is born again is born, not of blood, nor of the will of the flesh, nor of the will of man, but of God; for the Spirit is very God.

Beloved, this is a very humbling and awful truth. The conversion of a sinner can never be that light, offhand affair that some do seem to think it. This great change which must come over us can never be a thing so entirely within our reach and grasp that we may put off the old Adam like a cloak, and put on the new man, just when and where we please. Oh, but it is a work that cannot possibly be done without the hand of God! The same power which first created heaven and earth, and called the fair world around us into being—the same power alone can create in us new hearts, and renew in us right minds; the same power alone can convert the natural man into the spiritual.

Yes, you may dream of deathbed repentance, and say, By-and-by we will turn and become Christians; but you know not what you are saying: the softening of the hard heart, and the entrance upon new ways, and the taking up of new principles, is no such easy matter as you seem to fancy—it is work that can only be begun by power divine, and who shall say you may not put it off too long?

It is not the plainest and clearest preaching, however lovely it may sound, which can cause men to be born again, without the Spirit: you may set Paul to plant and Apollos to water, but the Spirit alone can give the increase; we may raise up congregations fair and formal, and sinews and flesh and skin may cover the dry bones— but until the Spirit breaths upon them they are no better than dead. Not all the wisdom of Solomon, not all the faith of Abraham, not all the prophecies of Isaiah, not all the eloquence of apostles, could avail to convert one single soul without the operation of the Holy Ghost. "Not by might, nor by power, but by my spirit, saith the Lord of hosts" (Zech. 4:6). And therefore I call this an awful truth. I know the Spirit is promised to all who ask it; but I tremble lest men should loiter and put off their souls' concerns so long that the Spirit may be grieved and leave them in their sins.

And still, beloved, awful as this truth may be to sinners, it is full of consolation to believers; it is full of sweet and unspeakable comfort to all who feel in themselves the holy workings of a new and spiritual nature. These can say with rejoicing, "It is not our right hand nor our arm which hath brought us on the way towards Zion; the Lord Himself was on our side; it was He who raised us from the death of sin to the life of righteousness, and surely He will never let us go. Once we were sleeping and dead in trespasses, but the Spirit awakened us and opened our eyes. We caught a sight of the punishment prepared for the ungodly; we heard a voice saying, 'Come unto me, and I will give you rest,' and we could sleep no longer. And surely we may hope that He, who graciously began the work of grace, will also carry it forward; He laid the foundation, and He will not let it decay; He began, and He will bring His handiwork to perfection.''

II. So much for the great cause and giver of the new birth—the Holy Spirit. It only remains for us to consider the means through which it is ordinarily conveyed, and comes, and the different ways and manners in which it generally shows itself and produces its wonderful effects.

Now, with respect to the means which the Holy Spirit doth ordinarily use, I would not have you for one minute suppose that I wish to limit or set bounds to the holy one of Israel. I do not for an instant deny that some have been born again without any outward visible machinery having been used—by a sort of secret impulse which cannot be well explained; but I do say that, generally speaking, the Holy Ghost, in giving to a man that blessed thing the new birth, is pleased to work upon his heart more or less by means which our eyes can see and which our minds can understand. I would not, then, have you ignorant that a man is seldom born again of the Spirit, without the *preaching of the gospel* having something to do in the change. This is a special instrument for turning men from darkness to light, and many a one can testify that it was through sermons he was first touched, and brought to the knowledge of the truth. It was Peter's preaching which first touched the men of Jerusalem after our Lord's death, insomuch that they were pricked to the heart and said, ''Men and brethren, what shall we do?'' It was the command which Jesus gave to the apostles before his ascension, they were ''to preach unto the people, and to testify'' (Acts 10:42). It was a cause of joy to Paul that Christ was preached at Rome: ''I therein do rejoice," he says, "and will rejoice" (Phil. 1:18). It was his own declaration about himself, "Christ sent me not to baptize, but to preach the gospel" (I Cor. 1:17). No means is so blessed in all the experience of Christ's church as the plain preaching of the gospel; no sign so sure of decay and rottenness in a church as the neglect of preaching; for there is no ordinance in which the Holy Spirit is so particularly present, none by which sinners are so often converted and brought back to God. Faith cometh by hearing; and how shall men believe except they hear? Therefore it is that we press upon you so continually to be diligent in hearing Christ preached; for none are so unlikely to be born again as those who will not listen to the truth.

And seldom, too, is a man born of the Spirit without the *Bible* having something to do in the work. The Bible was written by men who spake as they were moved by the Holy Ghost, and he who reads it seriously and attentively, or hears it read, is seeking acquaintance with God in God's own way. You would find few indeed among the Lord's true people who would not tell you that the starting point in their spiritual life was some saying or doctrine in Scripture; some part or portion, pressed home upon their consciences by an unseen, secret power, was among the first things which stirred them up to think and examine their ways; some plain declaration flashed across their minds and made them say, "If this be true I shall certainly be lost." Therefore it is we tell you over and over again, Search the Scriptures, search the Scriptures; they are the sword of the Spirit, they are the weapon by which the devil is often driven out; and he who leaves his Bible unread doth plainly not wish to be born again.

Once more. Never are men born of the Spirit without *prayer*. I believe there would not be found a single case of a person who had been quickened and made a new creature without God having been entreated of and inquired of before. Either he has prayed for himself, or some one has prayed for him: so Stephen died praying for his murderers, and by-and-by Saul was converted. The Lord loves to be sought after by His guilty creatures; and they who will not ask for the Holy Spirit to come down upon them have no right to expect in themselves any real change.

Such, then, beloved, are the means through which this new birth is generally given. I say generally, because it is not for me to set bounds to the operations of God; I know men may be startled by sicknesses and accidents and the like, but still I repeat that preaching, the Bible and prayer are the channels through which the Spirit ordinarily works. And I say further that in all my life and reading I never heard of a man who diligently, humbly, heartily, and earnestly made use of these means, who did not sooner or later find within himself new habits and principles; I never heard of a man steadily persevering in their use who did not sooner or later feel that sin and he must part company—who did not, in short, become a real child of God, a new creature.

III. So much for the means through which the Spirit generally conveys this new birth. There is yet one point to be considered this morning; and that is the *particular manner* in which this mighty spiritual change doth first touch a person and begin.

Now, on this point I remark, there are great diversities of operations; there is a vast variety in the methods by which the Spirit works, and hence it is that we can never say He is tied down to show Himself in one particular way; we must never condemn a person and tell him he is a graceless unconverted sinner because his experience may happen to differ widely from our own.

I would have you note, then, there is great diversity in the time and age at which this change begins. Some few have the grace of God in them from their very infancy; they are, as it were, sanctified and filled with the Holy Ghost from their mother's womb; they cannot so much as remember the time when they were without a deep sense of their natural corruption and a lively faith in Christ, and an earnest desire and endeavor to live close to God: such were Isaac and Samuel and Josiah and Jeremiah, and John the Baptist and Timothy. Blessed and happy are these souls; their memories are not saddened by the recollection of years wasted in carelessness and sin; their imaginations are not defiled and stained with the remembrance of youthful wickedness. But few indeed are to be found of this sort. There would be far more, I am persuaded, if infant baptism were not so inconsiderately and lightly regarded (as it too often is)—so scrambled over; but we have no reason to expect the children of unbelieving parents can turn out anything else but unclean and unholy; and when children are brought to the font without real faith and real prayer we have no warrant for supposing the baptism of water is accompanied by the baptism of the Holy Ghost. And let me also add that much depends on the education which parents give; and many a one could tell you he got his first impressions of religion from the teaching and example of a father and mother who really feared God.

But again. Many, perhaps the greater part of true Christians in our day, are never born of the Spirit till they come to age and have reached years of maturity. These were once walking after the course of this world, perhaps serving divers lusts and pleasures, perhaps decent outwardly and yet only regarding religion as a thing for Sundays, not as a concern of the hearts. But by some means or other God stops them in their career and turns their hearts back again, and they take up the cross. And bitter indeed is their repentance, and great is their wonder that they could have lived so long in such a fashion, and warm is the love they feel towards Him who has so graciously forgiven them all iniquity.

Once more. Some few, some very few, are first brought unto God and born again in the advance and in the decline of life. Oh, but it is fearful to see how few! There are not many who ever arrive at what is called old age; and of these I believe a very insignificant part indeed are ever brought to a saving change, if they have not been changed. And little wonder if we consider how deeply rooted a thing is habit, how hard it is for those who are accustomed to do evil to learn to do good. Oh, brethren beloved, youth is the time to seek the Lord! I know that with God nothing is impossible; I know that He can touch the rock that has long been unmoved, if He pleases, and make the water flow; but still we very seldom hear of old men or women being converted: gray hairs are the time for burning the oil of grace and not for buying it, and therefore I say, pray ye that your flight be not in the winter of life.

IV. The next thing I would have you note is the *great diversity in the ways* by which the Spirit, so to speak, doth strike the first blow in producing this new birth.

Some are awakened suddenly, by mighty providences and interpositions of God; they despise other warnings, and then the Lord comes in and violently shakes them out of sleep, and plucks them like brands from the burning. And this is often done by unexpected mercies, by extraordinary afflictions and troubles, by sicknesses, by accidents, by placing a man in some great danger and peril; and thousands, I am certain, will tell us in heaven, "It is good for us that we were tried and distressed; 'before I was afflicted I went astray, but now have I kept Thy word.' " This was the case with Paul: he was struck to the earth blinded, while going to Damascus to persecute, and he rose up a humbled and a wiser man. This was the case with Jonah: when he fled from the Lord's command, he was awakened by a storm while sleeping on board the ship. This was the case with Manasseh, king of Judah: he was taken prisoner and laid in chains at Babylon, and in his affliction he sought the Lord. This was the case with the jailer at Philippi: he was roused by the earthquake, and came and fell down, saying, "What shall I do to be saved?" This is the case spoken of by Elihu in the thirty-third of Job. And here is the reason why we ought to feel so anxious about a man, when God has laid His hand upon him and afflicted him. I always feel about such a person, "There is one whom the Lord is trying to convert: will it or will it not be all in vain?"

Again. Some are awakened suddenly, by very little and trifling things. God often raises up Christ's kingdom in a man's heart by a seed so small and insignificant, that all who see it are obliged to confess, "This is the Lord's doing, and it is marvelous in our eyes." A single text of Scripture sometimes; a few lines in a book taken up by accident; a chance expression or word dropped in conversation, and never perhaps meant by him who spoke it to do so much: each of these seeming trifles has been known to pierce men's hearts like an arrow, after sermons and ordinances have been used without appearing to avail. I have heard of one who could trace up the beginning of his conversion to the saying of a perfect stranger: he was profanely asking God to damn his soul, when the stranger stopped him and said it were better to pray that it might be blessed than damned; and that little word found its way to his heart. Oh, how careful should we be over our lips! Who knows what good might be done if we only strove more to speak a word in season?

Once more. Some are born of the Spirit gradually and insensibly. They hardly know at the period what is going on within them; they can hardly recollect any particular circumstances attending their conversion, or fix any particular time; but they do know this, that somehow or other they have gone through a great change, they do know that once they were careless about religion, and now they hold it chiefest in their affections: once they were blind and now they see. This seems to have been the case with Lydia at Philippi: the Lord gently opened her heart, so that she attended to the things spoken by Paul. This is what Elijah saw in the wilderness: there was the whirlwind and the earthquake and the fire, and after all there was something else—a still small voice. And here is one reason why we sometimes hope and trust that many amongst the hearers in our congregations may still prove children of God. We try to think that some of you feel more than you seem to do, and that the time is near when you will indeed come out and be separate, and not be ashamed to confess Christ before men.

There is one more diversity I would very shortly notice. Remember there is diversity in the feelings which the Spirit first excites: each feeling is moved sooner or later, but they are not moved always in the same order. The new birth shows itself in some by causing exceeding fear—they are filled with a strong sense of God's holiness, and they tremble because they have broken His law continually; others begin with sorrow—they can never mourn enough over their past wickedness and ingratitude; others begin with love—they are full of affection towards Him who died for them, and no sacrifice seems too great to make for His sake. But all these worketh one and the same Spirit; in this man He touches one string, and in that another; but sooner or later all are blended in harmony together, and when the new creation has fully taken place, fear and sorrow and love may all be found at once.

Beloved, time will not allow me to go further with this subject today. I have endeavored to show you this morning who is the worker, the cause of the new birth: it is not man, but God the Holy Ghost. What are the means through which He generally conveys it: preaching, the Bible, and prayer. And lastly I have shown you there are many diversities in His operations: with some He begins in infancy, with some in full years, with some few in old age. On some He comes down suddenly and on some gradually, in some He first moves one sort of feelings and in some another; but whatever be His operation, without the Spirit none can be born again.

And now, in conclusion, tell me not you mean to wait lazily and idly, and if the Lord gives you this blessed change, well, and if not you cannot help it. God does not deal with you as if you were machines or stones; He deals with you as those who can read and hear and pray, and this is the way in which He would have you wait upon Him. Never was doctrine so surrounded with promises and encouragements and invitations as this. Hear what Jeremiah says: "I will put my law in their inward parts, and write it in their hearts; and will be their God, and they shall be my people" (Jer. 31:33). Again: "They shall be my people, and I will be their God: and I will give them one heart, and one way, that they may fear me for ever, for the good of them, and of their children after them" (Jer. 32:38, 39). Then what Ezekiel says: "A new heart also will I give you, and a new spirit will I put within you: and I will take away the stony heart out of your flesh, and I will give you a heart of flesh. And I will put my spirit within you, and cause you to walk in my statutes" (Ezek. 36:26, 27). Then lastly what the Lord Jesus says: "Ask, and ye shall receive; seek, and ye shall find . . . every one that asketh receiveth . . . your heavenly Father shall give the Holy Spirit to them that ask him" (Luke 11:9, 10, 13). And this is what we want you to do: until you pray for yourselves in earnest, we know there will be little good done; and if any prayerless man shall say in the day of judgment, "I could not come to Christ," the answer will be, "You did not try."

Then quench not the Spirit, grieve not the Spirit, resist not the Spirit; His grace has been purchased for you. Strive and labor and pray that you may indeed receive it. And then God has covenanted and engaged that He shall come down like rain on the dry ground—like water to wash away your soul's defilement, like fire to burn away the dross and filth of sin, and the hardest heart among you shall become soft and willing as a weaned child.

We have reached the last point in our inquiry about the new birth—I mean the *marks* and *evidence* by which it may be known; the notes by which a man may find out whether he has himself been born again or no. To set before you the character of those who are indeed new creatures, to warn you against certain common mistakes respecting this doctrine, to wind up the whole subject by appealing to your consciences—this is the work which I propose to take in hand this morning.

Now this point may be last in order, but it certainly is not least in importance. It is the touchstone of our condition; it decides whether we are natural men or spiritual men, whether we are yet dead in trespasses, or have been quickened and brought to see the kingdom of God.

Many there are who take it for granted they have been born again—they do not exactly know why, but it is a sort of thing they never doubted; others there are who despise all such sifting inquiry—they are sure they are in the right way, they are confident they shall be saved, and as for marks, it is low and legal to talk about them, it is bringing men into bondage. But, beloved, whatever men may say, you may be certain Christ's people are a peculiar people, not only peculiar in their talk but peculiar in their life and conduct, and they may be distinguished from the unconverted around them; you may be certain there are stamps and marks and characters about God's handiwork by which it may always be known; and he who has got no evidences to show may well suspect that he is not in the right way.

Now, about these marks I can of course only speak very shortly and very generally, for time will not allow me to do more; but I would first say one word by way of caution. Remember, then, I would not have you suppose that all children of God do feel alike, or that these marks should be equally strong and plain in every case. The work of grace on man's heart is gradual: first the blade, then the ear, then the full corn in the ear. It is like leaven: the whole lump is not leavened at once. It is as in the birth of an infant into the world: first it feels, then moves and cries, and sees and hears and knows, and thinks and loves, and walks and talks and acts for itself. Each of these things comes gradually, and in order; but we do not wait for all before we say this is a living soul.

And just so is every one that is born of the Spirit. He may not, at first, find in himself all the marks of God, but he has the seed of them all about him; and some he knows by experience, and all, in the course of time, shall be known distinctly. But this at least you may be sure of: wherever there is no fruit of the Spirit, there is no work of the Spirit; and if any man have not the Spirit of Christ, he is none of His. Oh, that this question might stir up every one of you to search and try his ways! God is not a man that He should lie; He would not have given you the Bible if you could be saved without it; and here is a doctrine on which eternal life depends: "No salvation without the new birth."

I. First, then, and foremost, I would have you write down in your memories a mark which St. John mentions in his first epistle: "Whosoever is born of God doth not commit sin"; "whosoever is born of God sinneth not"; "whosoever abideth in him sinneth not: whosoever sinneth hath not seen him, neither known him" (I John 3:9; 5:18; 3:6).

Observe, I would not for one minute have you suppose that God's children are perfect, and without spot or stain or defilement in themselves. Do not go away and say I told you they were pure as angels and never made a slip or stumble. The same St. John in the same epistle declares: "If we say that we have no sin, we deceive ourselves, and the truth is not in us. . . . If we say that we have not sinned, we make him a liar, and his word is not in us" (I John 1:8, 10).

But I do say that in the matter of breaking God's commandments, every one that is born again is quite a new man. He no longer takes a light and cool and easy view of sin; he no longer judges of it with the world's judgment; he no longer thinks a little swearing, or a little Sabbath-breaking, or a little fornication, or a little drinking, or a little covetousness, small and trifling matters; but he looks on every sort of sin against God or man as exceeding abominable and damnable in the Lord's sight, and, as far as in him lies, he hates it and abhors it, and desires to be quit of it root and branch, with his whole heart and mind and soul and strength.

He that is born again has had the eyes of his understanding opened, and the Ten Commandments appear to him in an entirely new light. He feels amazed that he can have lived so long careless and indifferent about transgressions, and he looks back on the days gone by with shame and sorrow and grief. As for his daily conduct, he allows himself in no known sin; he makes no compromise with his old habits and his old principles; he gives them up unsparingly, though it cost him pain, though the world think him over-precise and a fool; but he is a new man, and will have nothing more to do with the accursed thing. I do not say but that he comes short, and finds his old nature continually opposing him—and this, too, when no eye can see it but his own; but then he mourns and repents bitterly over his own weakness. And this at least he has about him: he is at war, in reality, with the devil and all his works, and strives constantly to be free.

And do you call that no change? Look abroad on this world, this evil-doing world: mark how little men generally think about sin; how seldom they judge of it as the Bible does; how easy they suppose the way to heaven—and judge ye whether this mark be not exceeding rare. But for all this God will not be mocked, and men may rest assured that until they are convinced of the awful guilt and the awful power and the awful consequences of sin, and, being convinced, flee from it and give it up, they are most certainly not born again.

II. The second mark I would have you note is "faith in Christ," and here again I speak in the words of St. John in his first epistle: "Whosoever believeth that Jesus is the Christ is born of God" (I John 5:1).

I do not mean by this a general vague sort of belief that Jesus Christ once lived on earth and died—a sort of faith which the very devils possess; I mean, rather, that feeling which comes over a man when he is really convinced of his own guilt and unworthiness, and sees that Christ alone can be his Savior; when he becomes convinced he is in a way to be lost, and must have some righteousness better than his own, and joyfully embraces that righteousness which Jesus holds out to all who will believe. He that has got this faith discovers a fitness and suitableness and comfort in the doctrine of Christ crucified for sinners which once he never knew; he is no longer ashamed to confess himself by nature poor and blind and naked, and to take Christ for his only hope of salvation.

Before a man is born of the Spirit there seems no particular form nor comeliness about the Redeemer, but after that blessed change has taken place He appears the very chiefest in ten thousand: no honor so great but Jesus is worthy of it; no love so strong but on Jesus it is well bestowed; no spiritual necessity so great but Jesus can relieve it; no sin so black but Jesus' blood can wash it away. Before the new birth a man can bow at Christ's name, and sometimes wonder at Christ's miracles, but that is all; once born again, a man sees a fullness and a completeness and a sufficiency in Christ of things necessary to salvation, so that he feels as if he could never think upon Him enough. To cast the burden of sin on Jesus, to glory in the cross on which He died, to keep continually in sight His blood, His righteousness, His intercession, His mediation; to go continually to Him for peace and forgiveness, to rest entirely on Him for full and free salvation, to make Jesus, in short, all in all in their hopes of heaven—this is the most notable mark of all true children of God. They live by faith in Christ, in Christ their happiness is bound up.

It is the spiritual law of God which brings them to this: time was when they were ready to think well of themselves; the law strips off their miserable garments of self-righteousness, exposes their exceeding guilt and rottenness, cuts down to the ground their fancied notions of justification by their own works, and so leads them to Christ as their only wisdom and redemption; and then, when they have laid hold on Christ and taken Him for their Savior, they begin to find that rest which before they had sought in vain.

Such are two first marks of the Spirit's work—a deep conviction of sin and forsaking of it, and a lively faith in Christ crucified as the only hope of forgiveness—marks which the world perhaps may not see, but marks without which no man or woman was ever yet made a new creature. These are the two foundations of the Christian's character, the pillars, as it were, of the kingdom of God; they are hidden roots which others can only judge of by the fruit; but they who have them do generally know it, and can feel the witness in themselves.

III. The third mark of the new birth is "holiness." What says the apostle John again? "Every one that doeth righteousness is born of God"; "he that is begotten of God keepeth himself" (I John 2:29; 5:18).

The true children of God delight in making the law their rule of life; it dwells in their minds, and is written upon their hearts, and it is their meat and drink to do their Father's will. They know nothing of that spirit of bondage which false Christians complain of; it is their pleasure to glorify God with their bodies and souls, which are His; they hunger and thirst after tempers and dispositions like their Lord's. They do not rest content with sleepy wishing and hoping, but they strive to be holy in all manner of conversation—in thought, in word, and in deed; it is their daily heart's prayer, ''Lord what wilt thou have us to do?'' and it is their daily grief and lamentation that they come so short and are such unprofitable servants. Beloved, remember where there is no holiness of life there cannot be much work of the Holy Ghost.

IV. The fourth mark of the new birth is ''spiritual-mindedness.'' We learn this from St. Paul's words to the Colossians: ''If ye then be risen with Christ, seek those things which are above. . . . Set your affection on things above, not on things on the earth'' (Col. 3:1, 2).

He that is born again thinks first about the things which are eternal; he no longer gives up the best of his heart to this perishable world's concerns; he looks on earth as a place of pilgrimage, he looks on heaven as his home; and even as a child remembers with delight its absent parents, and hopes to be one day with them, so does the Christian think of his God and long for that day when he shall stand in His presence and go no more out. He cares not for the pleasures and amusements of the world around him; he minds not the things of the flesh, but the things of the Spirit; he feels that he has a house not made with hands eternal in the heavens, and he earnestly desires to be there. ''Lord,'' he says, ''whom have I in heaven but thee? and there is none upon earth that I desire beside thee'' (Ps. 73:25).

V. The fifth mark of the new birth is ''victory over the world.'' Hear what St. John says: ''Whosoever is born of

God overcometh the world: and this is the victory that overcometh the world, even our faith'' (I John 5:4).

What is the natural man?—a wretched slave to the opinion of this world. What the world says is right he follows and approves; what the world says is wrong he renounces and condemns also. How shall I do what my neighbors do not do? What will men say of me if I become more strict than they? This is the natural man's argument. But from all this he that is born again is free. He no longer is led by the praise or the blame, the laughter or the frown, of children of Adam like himself. He no longer thinks that the sort of religion which everybody about him professes must necessarily be right. He no longer considers ''What will the world say?'' but ''What does God command?'' Oh, it is a glorious change when a man thinks nothing of the difficulty of confessing Christ before men, in the hope that Christ will confess him and own him before the holy angels! That fear of the world is a terrible snare; with many thousands it far outweighs the fear of God. There are men who would care more for the laughter of a company of friends than they would for the testimony of half the Bible. From all this the spiritual man is free. He is no longer like a dead fish floating with the stream of earthly opinion; he is ever pressing upwards, looking unto Jesus in spite of all opposition. He has overcome the world.

VI. The sixth mark of the new birth is ''meekness.'' This is what David meant when he said, in Psalm 131:2, ''My soul is even as a weaned child.'' This is what our Lord has in view when He tells us we must ''be converted, and become as little children'' (Matt. 18:3).

Pride is the besetting sin of all natural men, and it comes out in a hundred different fashions. It was pride by which the angels fell and became devils. It is pride which brings many a sinner to the pit—he knows he is in the wrong about religion, but he is too proud to bend his neck and act up to what he knows. It is pride which may always be seen about false professors: they are always saying, "We are the men, and we are alone in the right, and ours is the sure way to heaven"; and by-and-by they fall and go to their own place and are heard no more of. But he that is born again is clothed with humility; he has a very childlike and contrite and broken spirit; he has a deep sense of his own weakness and sinfulness, and great fear of a fall. You never hear him professing confidence in himself and boasting of his own attainments—he is far more ready to doubt about his own salvation altogether and call himself "chief of sinners." He has no time to find fault with others, or be a busybody about his neighbors—enough for him to keep up the conflict with his own deceitful heart, the old Adam within. No enemy so bitter to him as his own inbred corruption. Whenever I see a man passing his time in picking holes in other churches, and talking about every one's soul except his own, I always feel in my own mind, "There is no work of the Spirit there." And it is just this humility and sense of weakness which makes God's children men of prayer. They feel their own wants and their danger, and they are constrained to go continually with supplication to Him who has given them the Spirit of adoption, crying, "Abba Father, help us and deliver us from evil."

VII. The seventh mark of the new birth is a "great delight in all means of grace." This is what Peter speaks of in his first epistle: "As newborn babes desire the sincere milk of the word, that ye may grow. . . ." (I Peter 2:2). This was the mind of David when he said, "A day in thy courts is better than a thousand. I had rather be a doorkeeper in the house of my God, than to dwell in the tents of wickedness'' (Ps. 84:10).

And, oh, what a difference there is between nature and grace in this matter! The natural man has often a form of godliness: he does not neglect the ordinances of religion, but somehow or other the weather, or his health, or the distance, contrives to be a great hindrance to him, and far too often it happens that the hours he spends in church or over his Bible are the dullest in his life.

But when a man is born again, he begins to find a reality about means which once he did not feel: the Sabbath no longer seems a dull, wearisome day, in which he knows not how to spend his time decently; he now calls it a delight and a privilege, holy of the Lord and honorable. The difficulties which once kept him from God's house now seem to have vanished away: dinner and weather and the like never detain him at home, and he is no longer glad of an excuse not to go. Sermons appear a thousand times more interesting than they used to do; and he would no more be inattentive or willingly go to sleep under them, than a prisoner would upon his trial. And, above all, the Bible looks to him like a new book. Time was when it was very dry reading to his mind—perhaps it lay in a corner dusty and seldom read—but now it is searched and examined as the very bread of life; many are the texts and passages which seem just written for his own case; and many are the days that he feels disposed to say with David, ''The law of thy mouth is better unto me than thousands of gold and silver'' (Ps. 119:72).

VIII. The eighth and last mark of the new birth is ''love towards others.'' ''Every one,'' says St. John, "that loveth is born of God, and knoweth God. He that loveth not knoweth not God; for God is love" (I John 4:7, 8).

He that is born of the Spirit loves his neighbor as himself; he knows nothing of the selfishness and uncharitableness and ill-nature of this world; he loves his neighbor's property as his own; he would not injure it, nor stand by and see it injured; he loves his neighbor's person as his own, and he would count no trouble ill-bestowed if he could help or assist him; he loves his neighbor's character as his own, and you will not hear him speak a word against it, or allow it to be blackened by falsehoods if he can defend it; and then he loves his neighbor's soul as his own, and he will not suffer him to turn his back on God without endeavoring to stop him by saying, "Oh, do not so!" Oh what a happy place would earth be if there was more love! Oh that men would only believe that the gospel secures the greatest comfort in the life that now is, as well as in the life to come!

And such, beloved, are the marks by which the new birth in a man's soul may generally be discovered. I have been obliged to speak of them very shortly, although each one of them deserves a sermon. I commend to your especial attention the two first: conviction and forsaking of sin, and faith in Christ; they are marks on which each must be his own judge. "Have I ever truly repented? Have I really closed with Christ and taken Him for my only Savior and Lord?" Let these questions be uppermost in your mind if you would know whether you are born again or not. The six last marks—viz., holiness, spiritual-mindedness, victory over the world, meekness, delight in means, and love—have this peculiarity about them, that a man's family and neighbors do often see more clearly whether he has got them than he does himself; but they all flow out of the two first, and therefore I once more urge the two first on your especial notice.

And now, brethren beloved, in concluding this course of sermons, I desire to speak one word to the consciences of all who have heard them: old or young, rich or poor, careless or thoughtful, you are all equally concerned.

For three Sunday mornings you have heard this new birth set before you according to my ability, and have you ever thought upon your own state and looked within? What of your own hearts? Are you living or dead, natural or spiritual, born again or not? Are your bodies temples of the Holy Ghost? Are your habits and characters the habits and characters of renewed creatures? Oh, search and see what there is within you: the language of the text is plain—no new birth, no kingdom of God.

I know there is nothing popular or agreeable about this doctrine; it strikes at the root of all compromising half-and-half religion, and still it is true. Many would like much to escape the punishment of sin, who will not strive to be free from its power; they wish to be justified by not to be sanctified; they desire much to have God's favor, but they care little for God's image and likeness; their talk is of pardon, but not of purity; they think much about God's willingness to forgive, but little about His warning that we be renewed. But this is leaving out of sight half the work which Christ died to perform: He died that we might become holy as well as happy, He purchased grace to sanctify as well as grace to redeem; and now forgiveness of sin and change of heart must never be separated. "What God hath joined together, let no man presume to put asunder" (Matt. 19:6). The foundation of God stands firm: "If any man have not the Spirit of Christ, he is none of his" (Rom. 8:9).

Beloved, it is easy work to live unto ourselves and take no trouble about religion; the world approves it, and says we shall probably do well at last; but if ever we are to be saved there is another life, and that too on this side the grave, we must live unto God. It is easy to be natural men—we give no offense, and the devil comforts us by saying, as he did to Eve, "Ye shall not surely die"; but the devil was a liar from the beginning. So long as we are natural men, we are dead already, and we must rise to newness of life. And what know ye of the movements of the Spirit? I ask not so much whether ye can say which way He came into your hearts, but I do ask whether ye can find any real footsteps or traces or tokens of His presence—for "if any man have not the Spirit of Christ, he is none of his."

Be not deceived and led away by false opinions. Head-knowledge is not the new birth: a man may know all mysteries like Balaam, and think his eyes are opened; or preach and work miracles and and be an apostle like Judas Iscariot, yet never be born again. Church membership is not the new birth; many do sit in churches and chapels who shall have no seat in Christ's kingdom; they are not Israel who have the circumcision of the flesh outwardly, they are the true Israel who have the circumcision of the heart, which is inward.

There were many Jews in the New Testament days who said, "We have Abraham for our father, and we have the temple among us and that is enough," but Jesus showed them that they only are Abraham's children who have the faith of Abraham and do Abraham's works. And then water baptism alone is not the new birth: it is the sign and seal, and when used with faith and prayer we have a right to look also for the baptism of the Holy Ghost; but to say that every man who has been baptized has been born again is contrary to Scripture and plain fact. Was not Simon Magus baptized? Yes, but Peter told him after his baptism that he was in the gall of bitterness and bond of iniquity, his heart not right in the sight of God. "I would not have you ignorant," says Paul to the Corinthians, "that all our fathers were baptized. . . . But with many of them God was not well pleased" (I Cor. 10:1, 2, 5). "Baptism," writes Peter, "doth also now save us"; but what baptism? "Not the putting away of the filth of the body, not the washing of water, but the answer of a pure conscience," a conscience made pure by the baptism of the Holy Ghost (I Peter 3:21).

Beloved, let no man lead you astray in this matter; let no man make you believe that a baptized drunkard or fornicator or blasphemer or worldling has been born of the Spirit; he has not the marks of the new birth, and he cannot have been born again; he is living in sin and carelessness, and St. John has given us his character— "He that committeth sin is of the devil" (I John 3:8). Remember, the outward seal is nothing without the inward writing on the heart. No evidence can be depended on excepting a new life and a new character and a new creature; and to say that men who want their evidences are born again is an unreasonable and unscriptural stretch of charity.

And now, in conclusion, if any one of you has reason to think that he still lacks this one thing needful, I entreat that man not to stifle his convictions or nip them in the bud. Do not go away like Cain and silence the voice of conscience by rushing into the vanities of the world, nor dream, like Felix, that you will have a more convenient season than the present; but remember, I tell you this day, there are two things which make a deathbed specially uncomfortable: first, purposes and promises not performed; and second, convictions slighted and not improved. And if any of you has satisfactory grounds for thinking that he has really tasted something of that saving and necessary change we have considered, I charge that man not to stand still, not to loiter, not to linger, not to look behind him; I warn him that none are in so dangerous a way as those who have become cool and cold and indifferent after real and warm concern about salvation; I urge him to press forward more and more towards the knowledge of Christ, and to remember it is a special mark of God's children that as they grow in age they grow in grace, and feel their sins more deeply and love their Lord and Savior more sincerely.

4
"Come unto Me"

"Come unto me, all ye that labor and are heavy laden, and I will give you rest."—Matt. 11:28

There are few texts more striking than this in all the Bible—few that contain so wide and sweeping an invitation—few that hold out so full and comfortable a promise.

Let us consider:

I. Who it is that speaks.
II. Who they are that are spoken to.
III. What is the invitation.
IV. What is the promise.

I. Who speaks? That is a most important question, and it is right to have it answered.

You live in a world of promise. "Come with us," says one party, and you will be rich. "Come with us," says another, and you will be happy.

The devil can promise. "Eat the forbidden fruit," he said to Eve, "and you shall be as gods, knowing good and evil. You shall never die" (Gen. 3:4, 5). But he lied to her.

87

The world can promise. "Sell all and embark for California," says one man, "and you will soon roll in wealth." "Invest all your money in railways," says another, "and you will soon make your fortune." I never take up a newspaper without seeing many alluring invitations. I see page after page of advertisements, all full of high-sounding promises. I read of short ways to health, wealth, and happiness, of all descriptions. But it is all words and nothing more, and so many a man finds.

But He that promises in our text is one who can be depended on. It is the Lord Jesus Christ, God's own Son.

He is *able* to do what He promises. He has all power in heaven and on earth. He has the keys of death and hell. The government is given to Him in time, and all judgment committed to Him in eternity.

He is *faithful* to do what He promises. He will not lie, nor deceive, nor break His promise. What He speaks that He will do, and what He undertakes that He will perform. Heaven and earth may pass away, but His word shall not pass away.

He is *willing* to do what He promises. He has long since proved this by the love He has shown to man, and the sacrifice He has made for man's soul. For man He came into the world; for man He suffered and died; for man He endured the cross and the shame. Surely He has a right to be believed.

Beloved brethren, see that you refuse not Him that speaketh to you this day. If a letter came to you from the ruler of this country you would not despise it. If you were sick, and advice came from a wise physician, you would not reject it. If you were in danger, and counsel came from your best and truest friend, you would not make light of it. Then hear the words that Jesus sends to you this day. Listen to the King of kings. Then body and soul shall be His.

II. Who are they that are spoken to? Jesus addresses the "laboring and heavy laden": "Come unto me all ye that labor and are heavy laden." Now, whom does this mean?

You must not fancy it describes the *poor in this world*. That would be a great mistake. It is possible to be poor in time and even poorer in eternity.

Nor yet must you fancy it describes the *sick and the afflicted*. That also is a great mistake. It is very possible to have trouble in this life and trouble in that to come— and this some of you may find.

The "laboring and heavy laden" describes all who are pressed down and burdened by a feeling of sin. It describes all whose consciences are set at work, and who are brought to concern about their soul—all who are anxious about salvation, and desire to have it—all who tremble at the thought of judgment, and know not how to get through it, and of hell, and are afraid of falling into it; and long for heaven, and dread not getting to it; and are distressed at the thought of their own badness, and want deliverance. All such persons appear to be the laboring and heavy laden to whom Jesus speaks.

This was the state of mind in which the Jews were to whom Peter preached on the day of Pentecost. Their consciences were awakened; they felt convinced and condemned; and when he had finished, we are told they said, "Men and brethren, what shall we do?" (Acts 2). This was the state of mind in which Saul was when Jesus met him going to Damascus, and smote him to the ground. A light seemed to break in on his mind. He got a sight of his one enormous sin and danger; and we read that, trembling and astonished, he said, "Lord, what wilt thou have me to do?" (Acts 9:6). This was the state of mind in which we see the jailer at Philippi. He was roused from sleep by an earthquake. His fear brought his sin to his remembrance, and he came and fell down before Paul and Silas, and said, "Sirs, what must I do to be saved?" (Acts 16:30).

This is the state of mind I desire to see in each of you, for the beginning of all saving religion. You will never come to Christ till you feel your need.

You *ought*, every one, to feel laboring and heavy laden. Truly it is a marvelous proof of man's corruption, that man can be so careless as they are. Many, I do believe, *feel something* of it, but never allow it. There are many aching hearts under silk and satin. There are many merry faces which only hide an uneasy conscience. All is not gold that glitters in happiness that seems like it. Few, I believe, are to be found who do not feel something of it *some time in their lives*. Halyburton said, not a soul in his parish, but once had conviction.

But to all laboring and heavy laden souls, whoever they may be, to you Jesus speaks—to you is this word of salvation sent. Take heed that it is not in vain.

Jesus speaks to *all* such: none are left out. Though you have been a persecutor like Saul, though a murderer like Manasseh, though a cheating extortioner like Zacchaeus, though unclean and profligate like the Magdalen, it matters nothing. Are you laboring and heavy laden? Then Jesus speaks to you. You may tell me, "I am such a sinner, Jesus never speaks to me." I answer, "It may be so; but are you laboring and heavy laden? Then Jesus speaks to you. You may say, "I am not fit." I see nothing said of fitness; I only see Jesus calling the laboring and heavy laden: if this is your case, He calls you. You may say, "I am not this—I am not converted." You do not know, perhaps; but are you laboring and heavy laden? Then Jesus is speaking to you.

Ah! brethren, I fear many of you know nothing of the state of the soul here spoken of. Your sins never cut you to the heart, or give you a moment's sorrow. You never really felt the confession of the church this day—"no health in us." You know nothing of communion with Christ. The remembrance of grievous burdens is not intolerable. You are satisfied with your present state: like Laodicea, "rich and increased with goods," comfortable and content. And what shall I say? I will say plainly, there is no hope for your soul while in such a state. I say if your soul is in such a state, better never have been born. Your hard heart must be broken. You must be brought to see your own guilt and danger, your eyes must be opened to understand your sinfulness. All who have entered heaven were once laboring and heavy laden; and except you are, you will never get there.

III. What is the invitation to the laboring and heavy laden? Jesus says, "Come unto me."

I love that word *come*. To me it seems full of grace, mercy, and encouragement. "Come now," says the Lord in Isaiah, "and let us reason together: though your sins be as scarlet, they shall be as white as snow" (Isa. 1:18).

Come is the word put in the mouth of the king's messenger in the parable of the guest-supper: "All is now ready: come unto the marriage" (Matt. 22:4).

Come is the last word in the Bible to sinners. "The Spirit and the bride say, Come" (Rev. 22:17).

Jesus does not say, "Go and get ready." This is the word of the Pharisee and self-righteous. "Go and work out a righteousness. Do this and that and be saved." Jesus says, "Come."

Jesus does not say, "Send." This is the poor Roman Catholic's word. "Put your soul in the hand of the priest. Commit your affairs to saints and angels, and not to Christ." Jesus says, "Come."

Jesus does not say, "Wait." This is the word of the enthusiast and the fanatic. "You can do nothing. You must not ask; you cannot pray; you must sit still." Cold comfort for troubled souls. Jesus says "Come."

Come is a word of *merciful invitation*. It seems to say, "I want you to escape the wrath to come. I am not willing that any should perish. I have no pleasure in death. I would fain have all men saved, and I offer all the water of life freely. So come to me."

Come is a word of *gracious expectation*. It seems to say, "I am here waiting for you. I sit on my mercy seat expecting you to come. I wait to be gracious. I wait for more sinners to come in before I close the door. I want more names written down in the book of life before it is closed for ever. So come to me."

Come is a word of *kind encouragement*. It seems to say, "I have got treasures to bestow if you will only receive them. I have that to give which makes it worth while to come: a free pardon, a robe of righteousness, a new heart, a star of peace. So come to me."

Brethren, I ask you to hear these words and lay them to heart. I plead for my Master; I stand here an ambassador; I ask you to come and be reconciled to God.

I ask you to *come with all your sins*, however many they may be. If you come to Him they will be taken away. I ask you *to come as you are*. You feel unfit; you say you are not good enough. The worse you think yourself, the better prepared you are. Christ is not a Savior of the fit, but of sinners. I ask you *to come now*. No other time is your own. The opportunity past, the door will be shut, and yourself dead. Come now. Come to Christ.

Ah! brethren, I fear that many of you will not take one saving step—will not come to Christ. You go on content with your own devices, like Balaam; like Felix, you never finally come to Christ.

I warn you plainly that you may come to church, and come to the table, and come to the minister, and yet never be saved. The one thing needed is actual coming to the Savior, actual coming to the fountain, actual washing in the blood of atonement. Except you do this, you will die in your sins.

Gird up your loins like a man, and resolve that you will come. Do you feel vile and unworthy to come? Tell it to Jesus. Do you feel as if you know not what to say and do when you come? Tell it to Jesus. Tell Him you are all sins; tell Him you are all weakness; tell Him you feel as if you had no faith and no power, no grace and no strength, no goodness and no love; but come to Him, and commit your soul to His charge. Let nothing keep you back from Christ.

Tell Him you have heard that He receiveth sinners; that you are such a one, and you want to be saved. Tell Him you have nothing to plead but His own word; but He said, "Come," and therefore you come to Him.

IV. Let us consider the promise held out: "I will give you rest."

Rest is a pleasant thing, and a thing that all seek after. The merchant, the banker, the tradesman, the soldier, the lawyer, the farmer, all look forward to the day when they shall be able to rest. But how few can find rest in this world! How many pass their lives in seeking it, and never seem able to reach it! It seems very near sometimes, and they fancy it will soon be their own. Some new event happens, and they are as far off rest as ever.

The whole world is full of restlessness and disappointment, weariness and emptiness. The very faces of worldly men let out the secret; their countenances give evidence that the Bible is true; they find no rest. "Vanity and vexation of spirit" is the true report of all here below. "Who will show us any good?" the bitter confession of many now, just as in David's time.

Take warning, young men and women. Think not that happiness is to be found in any earthly thing. Do not have to learn this by bitter experience. Realize it while young, and do not waste your time in hewing out "cisterns, broken cisterns, that can hold no water."

But Jesus offers rest to all who will come to Him. "Come unto me," he says, "and I will give you rest." He will give it. He will not *sell* it, as the Pharisee supposes—so much rest and peace in return for so many good works. He gives it freely to every coming sinner, without money and without price. He will not *lend*, as the Arminian supposes, so much peace and rest, all to be taken away by-and-by if we do not please Him; He gives it forever and for aye. His gifts are "without repentance."

"But what kind of rest will Jesus give me?" some men will say. "He will not give me freedom from labor and trouble. What kind of rest will He give?" Listen a few minutes, and I will tell you.

He will give you *rest from fear of sin*. The sins of the man who comes to Christ are completely taken away; they are forgiven, pardoned, removed, blotted out. They can no longer appear in condemnation against him. They are sunk in the depths of the sea. Ah! brethren, that is rest.

He will give you *rest from fear of law*. The law has no further claim on the man who has come to Christ. Its debts are all paid; its requirements are all satisfied.

Christ is the end of the law for righteousness. Christ has redeemed us from the curse of law. "Who shall lay any thing to the charge of God's elect in the day of judgment?" (Rom. 8:33). No believer can run his eye over the fifth chapter of Matthew, and not feel comforted. And that is rest.

He will give you *rest from fear of hell*. Hell cannot touch the man who has come to Christ. The punishment has been borne, the pain and suffering have been undergone by another, and he is free. And that, too, is rest.

He will give you *rest from fear of the devil*. The devil is mighty, but he cannot touch those who have come to Christ. Their Redeemer is strong. He will set a hedge around them that Satan cannot overthrow. He may sift and buffet and vex, but he cannot destroy such. And that, too, is rest.

He will give you *rest from fear of death*. The sting of death is taken away when a man comes to Christ. Jesus has overcome death, and it is a conquered enemy. The grave loses half its terrors when we think it is "the place where the Lord lay." The believer's soul is safe whatever happens to his body. His flesh rests in hope. This also is rest.

He will give you *rest in the storm of affliction*. He will comfort you with comfort the world knows nothing of. He will cheer your heart, and sustain your fainting spirit. He will enable you to bear loss patiently, and to hold your peace in the day of wrath. Oh! this is rest indeed.

I know well, brethren, that believers do not enjoy so much rest as they might. I know well that they "bring a bad report of the land," and live below their privileges. It is their unbelief; it is their indwelling sin. There was a well near Hagar, but she never saw it. There was safety for Peter on the water, but he did not look to Jesus, and was afraid. And just so it is with many believers: they give way to needless fear—are straitened in themselves.

But still there is a real rest and peace in Christ for all who come to Him. The man that fled to the city of refuge was safe when once within the walls, though perhaps at first he hardly believed it; and so it is with the believer.

And, after all, the most downcast and complaining child of God has got something within him he would not exchange for all the world. I never met with one, however low and desponding, who would consent to part with the rest and peace he had, however small. Like Naboth he prizes his little vineyard like a kingdom. And this shows me that coming to Christ can give rest.

Be advised, every one of you who is now seeking rest in the world. Be advised, and come and seek rest in Christ. You have no home, no refuge, no hiding-place, no portion. Sickness and death will soon be upon you, and you are unprepared. Be advised, and seek rest in Christ. There is enough in Him and to spare. Who has tried and did not find? A dying Welsh boy said, in broken English, "Jesus Christ plenty for everybody." Know your privileges, all you who have come to Christ. You have something solid under foot and something firm under hand. You have a rest even now, and you shall have more abundantly.

Let me speak to *those who have not yet come to Christ.*

Why do you not come? What possible reason can you give? What excuse can you show for your present conduct?

Will you tell me you have no need? What! no sin to be pardoned—no iniquity to be covered over! There is no state so bad as that of utter insensibility. Beware, lest you only awake to hear the word, "Depart."

Will you tell me you are happy without Christ? I do not believe you. I know you are not. You dare not look into your heart, you dare not search your conscience. It is the happiness of a tradesman who is bankrupt and does not look at his books. There is no happiness out of Christ.

Take heed. Every morning you are in awful danger. You stand on the brink of hell. Let a fever, an accident, an attack of disease carry you off, and you are lost forever. Oh! take the warning. Escape for your life. Flee, flee to Christ!

Let me speak to those *who have not come to Christ, but mean to some day*. I marvel at your presumption. Who are you, that talk of meaning? You may be dead in a week. Who are you that talk of meaning? You may never have the will or opportunity, if not today. How long will you go on halting between two opinions? You must come to Christ some time—some day; why not now? The longer you stay away, the less chance there is of your coming at all; and the less happiness will you have in the world.

"Take heed, therefore, lest, a promise being left us of entering into His rest, any of you should seem to come short of it."

Many meant to have come in the robes, but put it off till too late. If like the Levite you put off your journey till late in the day, you must not wonder if the sun has gone down when you are far from home. Come now.

Let me speak to *those who have come to Christ indeed*.

You are often cast down and disquieted within you. And why? Just because you do not abide in Christ and seek all rest and peace in Him. You wander from the fold; no wonder you return weary, footsore, and tired. Come again to the Lord Jesus and renew the covenant. Believe me, if you live to be as old as Methuselah, you will never get beyond this: a sinner saved by the grace of Christ. And think of the sinner's end.

Rest in Christ, and so rest indeed.

5

Prayer

"Men ought always to pray."—Luke 18:1
"I will that men pray every where."—I Tim. 2:8

Prayer is the most important subject in practical religion. All other subjects are second to it. Reading the Bible, keeping the Sabbath, hearing sermons, attending public worship, going to the Lord's Table—all these are very weighty matters. But none of them are so important as private prayer.

I propose in this paper to offer seven plain reasons why I use such strong language about prayer. I invite to these reasons the attention of every thinking man into whose hands this paper may fall. I venture to assert with confidence that they deserve serious consideration.

I. In the first place, *prayer is absolutely needful to a man's salvation.*

I say absolutely needful, and I say so advisedly. I am not speaking now of infants and idiots. I am not settling the state of the heathen. I remember that where little is given, there little will be required. I speak especially of those who call themselves Christians, in a land like our own. And of such I say no man or woman can expect to be saved who does not pray.

I hold salvation by grace as strongly as anyone. I would gladly offer a free and full pardon to the greatest sinner that ever lived. I would not hesitate to stand by his dying bed, and say, "Believe on the Lord Jesus Christ even now, and you shall be saved." But that a man can have salvation without *asking* for it, I cannot see in the Bible. That a man will receive pardon of his sins, who will not so much as lift up his heart inwardly, and say, "Lord Jesus, give it to me," this I cannot find. I can find that nobody will be saved by his prayers, but I cannot find that without prayer anybody will be saved.

It is not absolutely needful to salvation that a man should *read* the Bible. A man may have no learning, or be blind, and yet have Christ in his heart. It is not absolutely needful that a man should *hear* the public preaching of the gospel. He may live where the gospel is not preached, or he may be bedridden, or deaf. But the same thing cannot be said about prayer. It is absolutely needful to salvation that a man should *pray*.

There is no royal road either to health or learning. Princes and kings, poor men and peasants, all alike must attend to the wants of their own bodies and their own minds. No man can eat, drink, or sleep by proxy. No man can get the alphabet learned for him by another. All these are things which everybody must do for himself, or they will not be done at all.

Just as it is with the mind and body, so it is with the soul. There are certain things absolutely needful to the soul's health and well-being. Each one must attend to these things for himself. Each must repent for himself. Each must apply to Christ for himself. And for himself each one must speak to God and pray. You must do it for yourself, for by nobody else can it be done.

How can we expect to be saved by an "unknown" God? And how can we know God without prayer? We know nothing of men and women in this world, unless we speak with them. We cannot know God in Christ, unless we speak to Him in prayer. If we wish to be with Him in heaven, we must be His friends on earth. If we wish to be His friends on earth, *we must pray.*

There will be many at Christ's right hand in the last day. The saints gathered from north and south, and east and west, will be "a multitude that no man can number" (Rev. 7:9). The song of victory that will burst from their mouths, when their redemption is at length complete, will be a glorious song indeed. It will be far above the noise of many waters, and of mighty thunders. But there will no discord in that song. They that sing will sing with one heart as well as one voice. Their experience will be one and the same. All will have believed. All will have been washed in the blood of Christ. All will have been born again. All will have prayed. Yes, we must pray on earth, or we shall never praise in heaven. We must go through the school of prayer, or we shall never be fit for the holiday of praise. In short, to be prayerless is to be without God—without Christ—without grace—without hope—and without heaven. It is to be in the road to hell.

II. In the second place, *a habit of prayer is one of the surest marks of a true Christian.*

All the children of God on earth are alike in this respect. From the moment there is any life and reality about their religion, they pray. Just as the first sign of life in an infant when born into the world, is the act of breathing, so the first act of men and women when they are born again, is *praying.*

This is one of the common marks of all the elect of God: "They cry unto him day and night" (Luke 18:7). The Holy Spirit, who makes them new creatures, works in them the feeling of adoption, and makes them cry, "Abba, Father" (Rom. 8:15). The Lord Jesus, when He quickens them, gives them a voice and a tongue, and says to them, "Be dumb no more." God has no dumb children. It is as much a part of their new nature to pray, as it is of a child to cry. They see their need of mercy and grace. They feel their emptiness and weakness. They cannot do otherwise than they do. They *must* pray.

I have looked carefully over the lives of God's saints in the Bible. I cannot find one of whose history much is told us, from Genesis to Revelation, who was not a man of prayer. I find it mentioned as a characteristic of the godly, that "they call on the Father," that "they call on the name of the Lord Jesus Christ." I find it recorded as a characteristic of the wicked, that "they call not upon the Lord" (I Peter 1:17; I Cor. 1:2; Ps. 14:4).

I have read the lives of many eminent Christians who have been on earth since the Bible days. Some of them, I see, were rich, and some poor. Some were learned, and some unlearned. Some of them were Episcopalians, some Presbyterians, some Baptists, some Independents. Some were Calvinists, and some Arminians. Some have loved to use a liturgy, and some to use none. But one thing, I see, they all have in common. They have all been *men of prayer*.

I study the reports of missionary societies in our own times. I see with joy that heathen men and women are receiving the gospel in various parts of the globe. There are conversions in Africa, in New Zealand, in Hindostan, in America. The people converted are naturally unlike one another in every respect. But one striking thing I observe at all the missionary stations. The converted people *always pray*.

I do not deny that a man may pray without heart, and without sincerity. I do not for a moment pretend to say that the mere fact of a person praying proves everything about his soul. As in every other part of religion, so also in this, there is plenty of deception and hypocrisy.

But this I do say—that not praying is a clear proof that a man is not yet a true Christian. He cannot really feel his sins. He cannot love God. He cannot feel himself a debtor to Christ. He cannot long after holiness. He cannot desire heaven. He has yet to be born again. He has yet to be made a new creature. He may boast confidently of election, grace, faith, hope, and knowledge, and deceive ignorant people. But you may rest assured it is all vain talk *if he does not pray*.

And I say furthermore, that of all the evidences of real work of the Spirit, a habit of hearty private prayer is one of the most satisfactory that can be named. A man may preach from false motives. A man may write books, and make fine speeches, and seem diligent in good works, and yet be a Judas Iscariot. But a man seldom goes into his closet, and pours out his soul before God in secret, unless he is in earnest. The Lord Himself has set His stamp on prayer as the best proof of a true conversion. When He sent Ananias to Saul in Damascus, He gave him no other evidence of his change of heart than this—*"Behold, he prayeth"* (Acts 9:11).

I know that much may go on in a man's mind before he is brought to pray. He may have many convictions, desires, wishes, feelings, intentions, resolutions, hopes, and fears. But all these things are very uncertain evidences. They are to be found in ungodly people, and often come to nothing. In many a case they are not more lasting than "the morning cloud, and the dew that goeth away" (Hos. 6:4). A real hearty prayer, flowing from a broken and contrite spirit, is worth all these things put together.

I know that the elect of God are chosen to salvation from all eternity. I do not forget that the Holy Spirit, who calls them in due time, in many instances leads them by very slow degrees to acquaintance with Christ. But the eye of man can only judge by what it sees. I cannot call any one justified until he believes. I dare not say that any one believes until he prays. I cannot understand a dumb faith. The first act of faith will be to speak to God. Faith is to the soul what life is to the body. Prayer is to faith what breath is to life. How a man can live and not breathe is past my comprehension, and how a man can believe and not pray is past my comprehension too.

Let no one be surprised if he hears ministers of the gospel dwelling much on the importance of prayer. This is the point we want to bring you to—we want to know that you pray. Your views of doctrine may be correct. Your love of Protestantism may be warm and unmistakeable. But still this may be nothing more than head knowledge and party spirit. The great point is this—whether you can speak *to* God as well as speak *about* God.

III. In the third place, *there is no duty in religion so neglected as private prayer*.

We live in days of abounding religious profession. There are more places of public worship now than there ever were before. There are more persons attending them than ever have been since England was a nation. And yet in spite of all this public religion, I believe there is a vast neglect of private prayer.

I should not have said so a few years ago. I once thought, in my ignorance, that most people said their prayers, and many people prayed. I have lived to think differently. I have come to the conclusion that the great majority of professing Christians do not pray at all.

I know this sounds very shocking, and will startle many. But I am satisfied that prayer is just one of those things which is thought a "matter of course," and, like many matters of course, is shamefully neglected. It is "everybody's business"; and, as it often happens in such cases, it is a business carried on by very few. It is one of those private transactions between God and our souls which no eye sees, and therefore one which there is every temptation to pass over and leave undone.

I believe that thousands *never say a word of prayer at all*. They eat; they drink; they sleep; they rise; they go forth to their labor; they return to their homes; they breathe God's air; they see God's sun; they walk on God's earth; they enjoy God's mercies; they have dying bodies; they have judgment and eternity before them. But they *never speak to God!* They live like the beasts that perish; they behave like creatures without souls; they have not a word to say to Him in whose hand are their life, and breath, and all things, and from whose mouth they must one day receive their everlasting sentence. How dreadful this seems! But if the secrets of men were only known, how common!

I believe there are tens of thousands *whose prayers are nothing but a mere form*—a set of words repeated by rote, without a thought about their meaning. Some say over a few hasty sentences picked up in the nursery when they were children. Some content themselves with repeating the belief, forgetting that there is not a request in it. Some add the Lord's Prayer, but without the slightest desire that its solemn petitions may be granted. Some among the poor, even at this day, repeat the old popish lines:

> Matthew, Mark, Luke, and John,
> Bless the bed that I lie on.

Many, even of those who use good forms, mutter their prayers over after they have got into bed, or scramble over them while they wash or dress in the morning. Men may think what they please, but they may depend that in the sight of God *this is not praying*. Words said without heart are as utterly useless to our souls as the drum-beating of the poor heathen before their idols. Where there is *no heart*, there may be lip-work and tongue-work, but there is nothing that God listens to— there is *no prayer*. Saul, I have no doubt, said many a long prayer before the Lord met him on the way to Damascus. But it was not till his heart was broken that the Lord said, ''He prayeth.''

Does this surprise any reader? Listen to me and I will show you that I am not speaking as I do without reason. Do you think that my assertions are extravagant and unwarrantable? Give me your attention, and I will soon show you that I am only telling you the truth.

Have you forgotten that it is *not natural* to any one to pray? The carnal mind is enmity against God. The desire of man's heart is to get far away from God, and to have nothing to do with Him. His feeling toward Him is not love but fear. Why then should a man pray when he has no real sense of sin, no real feeling of spiritual wants, no thorough belief in unseen things, no desire after holiness and heaven? Of all these things the vast majority of men know and feel nothing. The multitude walk in the broad way. I cannot forget this. Therefore I say boldly, I believe that few pray.

Have you forgotten that it is *not fashionable* to pray? It is just one of the things that many would be rather ashamed to own. There are hundreds who would sooner storm a breach, or lead a forlorn hope, than confess publicly that they make a habit of prayer. There are thousands who, if obliged by chance to sleep in the same room with a stranger, would lie down in bed without a prayer. To ride well, to shoot well, to dress well, to go to balls, and concerts, and theaters, to be thought clever and agreeable—all this is fashionable, but not to pray. I cannot forget this. I cannot think a habit is common which so many seem ashamed to own. I believe that few pray.

Have you forgotten *the lives that many live?* Can we really suppose that people are praying against sin night and day, when we see them plunging right into it? Can we suppose they pray against the world, when they are entirely absorbed and taken up with its pursuits? Can we think they really ask God for grace to serve Him, when they do not show the slightest desire to serve Him at all? Oh, no! It is plain as daylight that the great majority of men either ask nothing of God, or *do not mean what they say* when they do ask—which is just the same thing. Praying and sinning will never live together in the same heart. Prayer will consume sin, or sin will choke prayer. I cannot forget this. I look at men's lives. I believe that few pray.

Have you forgotten *the deaths that many die?* How many, when they draw near death, seem entirely strangers to God. Not only are they sadly ignorant of His gospel, but sadly wanting in the power of speaking to Him. There is a terrible awkwardness, and shyness, and newness, and rawness, in their endeavors to approach Him. They seem to be taking up a fresh thing. They appear as if they wanted an introduction to God, and as if they had never talked with him before. I remember having heard of a lady who was anxious to have a minister to visit her in her last illness. She desired that he would pray with her. He asked her what he should pray for. She did not know and could not tell. She was utterly unable to name any one thing which she wished him to ask God for her soul. All she seemed to want was the form of a minister's prayers. I can quite understand this. Death-beds are great revealers of secrets. I cannot forget what I have seen of sick and dying people. This also leads me to believe that few pray.

IV. In the fourth place, *prayer is that act in religion to which there is the greatest encouragement*.

There is everything on God's part to make prayer easy, if men will only attempt it. "All things are ready" on His side. (Luke 14:17). Every objection is antici-pated. Every difficulty is provided for. The crooked places are made straight, and the rough places are made smooth. There is no excuse left for the prayerless man.

There is *a way* by which any man, however sinful and unworthy, may draw near to God the Father. Jesus Christ has opened that way by the sacrifice He made for us upon the cross. The holiness and justice of God need not frighten sinners and keep them back. Only let them cry to God in the name of Jesus—only let them plead the atoning blood of Jesus—and they shall find God upon a throne of grace, willing and ready to hear. The name of Jesus is a never-failing passport to our prayers. In that name a man may draw near to God with boldness, and ask with confidence. God has engaged to hear him. Think of this. Is not this encouragement?

There is *an advocate* and intercessor always waiting to present the prayers of those who will employ Him. That advocate is Jesus Christ. He mingles our prayers with the incense of His own almighty intercession. So mingled they go up as a sweet savor before the throne of God. Poor as they are in themselves, they are mighty and powerful in the hand of our High Priest and elder brother. The bank note without a signature at the bottom is nothing but a worthless piece of paper. A few strokes of a pen confer on it all its value. The prayer of a poor child of Adam is a feeble thing in itself, but once endorsed by the hand of the Lord Jesus it availeth much. There was an officer in the city of Rome who was appointed to have his doors always open, in order to receive any Roman citizen who applied to him for help. Just so the ear of the Lord Jesus is ever open to the cry of all who want mercy and grace. It is His office to help them. Their prayer is His delight. Think of this. Is not this encouragement?

There is *the Holy Spirit* ever ready to help our infirmities in prayer. It is one part of His special office to assist us in our endeavors to speak to God. We need not be cast down and distressed by the fear of not knowing what to say. The Spirit will give us words if we will only seek His aid. He will supply us with ''thoughts that breathe and words that burn.'' The prayers of the Lord's people are the inspiration of the Lord's Spirit—the work of the Holy Ghost who dwells within them as the Spirit of grace and supplications. Surely the Lord's people may well hope to be heard. It is not they merely that pray, but the Holy Ghost pleading in them (Rom. 8:26). Think of this. Is not this encouragement?

There are exceeding great and precious *promises* to those who pray. What did the Lord Jesus mean when He spoke such words as these, ''Ask, and it shall be given you; seek, and ye shall find; knock, and it shall be opened unto you: for every one that asketh receiveth; and he that seeketh findeth; and to him that knocketh it shall be opened" (Matt. 7:7, 8). "All things, whatsoever ye shall ask in prayer, believing, ye shall receive" (Matt. 21:22). "Whatsoever ye shall ask in my name, that will I do, that the Father may be glorified in the Son. If ye shall ask any thing in my name, I will do it" (John 14:13, 14). What did the Lord mean when He spoke the parables of the friend at midnight and the importunate window? (Luke 11:5-8; 18:1-9). Think over these passages. If this is not encouragement to pray, words have no meaning at all.

There are wonderful *examples* in Scripture of the power of prayer. Nothing seems to be too great, too hard, or too difficult for prayer to do. It has obtained things that seemed impossible and out of reach. It has won victories over fire, air, earth, and water. Prayer opened the Red Sea. Prayer brought water from the rock and bread from heaven. Prayer made the sun stand still. Prayer brought fire from the sky on Elijah's sacrifice. Prayer turned the counsel of Ahithophel into foolishness. Prayer overthrew the army of Sennacherib. Well might Mary, Queen of Scots, say, "I fear John Knox's prayers more than an army of ten thousand men." Prayer has healed the sick. Prayer has raised the dead. Prayer has procured the conversion of souls. "The child of many prayers," said an old Christian to Augustine's mother, "shall never perish." Prayer, pains, and faith can do anything. Nothing seems impossible when a man has the Spirit of adoption. "Let me alone," is the remarkable saying of God to Moses, when Moses was about to intercede for the children of Israel (Exod. 32:10). The Chaldee version has it "Leave off praying." So long as Abraham asked mercy for Sodom, the Lord went on giving. He never ceased to give till Abraham ceased to pray. Think of this. Is not this encouragement?

What more can a man want to lead him to take any step in religion than the things I have just told him about prayer? What more could be done to make the path to the mercy seat easy, and to remove all occasions of stumbling from the sinner's way? Surely if the devils in hell had such a door set open before them they would leap for gladness, and make the very pit ring with joy.

But where will the man hide his head at last who neglects such glorious encouragements? What can be possibly said for the man who after all dies without prayer? God forbid that any reader of this paper should be that man.

V. In the fifth place, *diligence in prayer is the secret of eminent holiness.*

Without controversy there is a vast difference among true Christians. There is an immense interval between the foremost and the hindermost in the army of God.

They are all fighting the same good fight; but how much more valiantly some fight than others! They are all doing the Lord's work; but how much more some do than others! They are all light in the Lord; but how much more brightly some shine than others! They are all running the same race; but how much faster some get on than others! They all love the same Lord and Savior; but how much more some love Him than others! I ask any true Christian whether this is not the case. Are not these things so?

There are some of the Lord's people who seem *never able to get on* from the time of their conversion. They are born again, but they remain babies all their lives. They are learners in Christ's school, but they never seem to get beyond A B C, and the lowest form. They have got inside the fold, but there they lie down and get no further. Year after year you see in them the same old besetting sins. You hear from them the same old experience. You remark in them the same want of spiritual appetite, the same squeamishness about anything but the milk of the Word, and the same dislike to strong meat, the same childishness, the same feebleness, the same littleness of mind, the same narrowness of heart, the same want of interest in anything beyond their own little circle, which you remarked ten years ago. They are pilgrims indeed, but pilgrims like the Gibeonites of old—their bread is always dry and moldy, their shoes always old and clouted, and their garments always rent and torn (Josh. 9:4, 5). I say this with sorrow and grief. But I ask any real Christian, Is it not true?

There are others of the Lord's people who seem to be *always getting on*. They grow like the grass after rain. They increase like Israel in Egypt. They press on like Gideon—though sometimes "faint, yet always pursuing" (Judg. 8:4). They are ever adding grace to grace, and faith to faith, and strength to strength. Every time you meet them their hearts seem larger, and their spiritual stature bigger, taller, and stronger. Every year they appear to see more, and know more, and believe more, and feel more in their religion. They not only have good works to prove the reality of their faith, but they are *zealous* of them. They not only do well, but they are *unwearied* in well-doing (Titus 2:14; Gal. 6:9). They attempt great things, and they do great things. When they fail they try again, and when they fall they are soon up again. And all this time they think themselves poor unprofitable servants, and fancy they do nothing at all! These are those who make religion lovely and beautiful in the eyes of all. They wrest praise even from the unconverted, and win golden opinions even from the selfish men of the world. These are those whom it does one good to see, to be with, and to hear. When you meet them, you could believe that, like Moses, they had just come out from the presence of God. When you part with them you feel warmed by their company, as if your soul had been near a fire. I know such people are rare. I only ask, Is it not so?

Now, how can we account for the difference which I have just described? What is the reason that some believers are so much brighter and holier than others? I believe the difference, in nineteen cases out of twenty, arises from different habits about private prayer. I believe that those who are not eminently holy pray *little*, and those who are eminently holy pray *much*.

I daresay this opinion will startle some readers. I have little doubt that many look on eminent holiness as a kind of special gift, which none but a few must pretend to aim at. They admire it at a distance, in books: they think it beautiful when they see an example near themselves. But as to its being a thing within the reach of any but a very few, such a notion never seems to enter their minds. In short, they consider it a kind of monopoly granted to a few favored believers, but certainly not to all.

Now I believe that this is a most dangerous mistake. I believe that spiritual, as well as natural, greatness, depends far more on the use of means within everybody's reach, than on anything else. Of course I do not say we have a right to expect a miraculous grant of intellectual gifts. But this I do say, that when a man is once converted to God, whether he shall be eminently holy or not depends chiefly on his own diligence in the use of God's appointed means. And I assert confidently, that the principal means by which most believers have become great in the church of Christ is the habit of *diligent private prayer*.

Look through the lives of the brightest and best of God's servants, whether in the Bible or not. See what is written of Moses, and David, and Daniel, and Paul. Mark what is recorded of Luther and Bradford, the Reformers. Observe what is related of the private devotions of Whitefield, and Cecil, and Venn, and Bickersteth, and McCheyne. Tell me of one of all the goodly fellowship of saints and martyrs, who has not had this mark most prominently—he was *a man of prayer*. Oh, depend upon it, prayer is power!

Prayer obtains fresh and continued outpourings of the Spirit. He alone begins the work of grace in a man's heart; He alone can carry it forward and make it prosper. But the good Spirit loves to be entreated. And those who ask most, will always have most of His influence.

Prayer is the surest remedy against the devil and besetting sins. That sin will never stand firm which is heartily prayed against; that devil will never long keep dominion over us which we beseech the Lord to cast forth. But, then, we must spread out all our case before our heavenly physician, if He is to give us daily relief: we must drag our indwelling devils to the feet of Christ, and cry to Him to send them back to the pit.

Do we wish to grow in grace and be very holy Christians? Then let us never forget the value of prayer.

VI. In the sixth place, *neglect of prayer is one great cause of backsliding*.

There is such a thing as going back in religion, after making a good profession. Men may run well for a season, like the Galatians, and then turn aside after false teachers. Men may profess loudly, while their feelings are warm, as Peter did; and then, in the hour of trial, deny their Lord. Men may lose their first love, as the Ephesians did. Men may cool down in their zeal to do good, like Mark, the companion of Paul. Men may follow an apostle for a season, and then, like Demas, go back to the world. All these things men may do.

It is a miserable thing to be a backslider. Of all unhappy things that can befall a man, I suppose it is the worst. A stranded ship, a broken-winged eagle, a garden overrun with weeds, a harp without strings, a church in ruins—all these are sad sights; but a backslider is a sadder sight still. That true grace shall never be extinguished, and true union with Christ never be broken off, I feel no doubt. But I do believe that a man may fall away so far that he shall lose sight of his own grace, and despair of his own salvation. And if this is not hell, it is certainly the next thing to it! A wounded conscience, a mind sick of itself, a memory full of self-reproach, a heart pierced through with the Lord's arrows, a spirit broken with a load of inward accusation—all this is *a taste of hell*. It is a hell on earth. Truly that saying of the wise man is solemn and weighty, ''The backslider in heart shall be filled with his own ways'' (Prov. 14:14).

Now, what is the cause of most backsliding? I believe, as a general rule, one of the chief causes is neglect of private prayer. Of course the secret history of falls will not be known till the last day. I can only give my opinion as a minister of Christ and a student of the heart. That opinion is, I repeat distinctly, that backsliding generally first begins with *neglect of private prayer*.

Bibles read without prayer, sermons heard without prayer, marriages contracted without prayer, journeys undertaken without prayer, residences chosen without prayer, friendships formed without prayer, the daily act of private prayer itself hurried over or gone through without heart—these are the kind of downward steps by which many a Christian descends to a condition of spiritual palsy, or reaches the point where God allows him to have a tremendous fall.

This is the process which forms the lingering Lots, the unstable Samsons, the wife-idolizing Solomons, the inconsistent Asas, the pliable Jehoshaphats, the over-careful Marthas, of whom so many are to be found in the church of Christ. Often the simple history of such cases is this—they became *careless about private prayer*.

We may be very sure that men fall in private long before they fall in public. They are backsliders on their knees long before they backslide openly in the eyes of the world. Like Peter, they first disregard the Lord's warning to watch and pray; and then, like Peter, their strength is gone, and in the hour of temptation they deny their Lord.

The world takes notice of their fall, and scoffs loudly. But the world knows nothing of the real reason. The heathen succeeded in making Origen, the old Christian father, offer incense to an idol, by threatening him with a punishment worse than death. They then triumphed greatly at the sight of his cowardice and apostasy. But the heathen did not know the fact, which Origen himself tells us, that on that very morning he had left his bedchamber hastily, and without finishing his usual prayers.

If any reader of this paper is a Christian indeed I trust he will never be a backslider. But if you do not wish to be a backsliding Christian, remember the hint I give you— Mind your prayers.

VII. In the seventh place, *prayer is one of the best receipts for happiness and contentment*.

We live in a world where sorrow abounds. This has always been its state since sin came in. There cannot be sin without sorrow. And till sin is driven out from the world it is vain for any one to suppose he can escape sorrow.

Some, without doubt, have a larger cup of sorrow to drink than others. But few are to be found who live long without sorrows or cares of one sort or another. Our bodies, our property, our families, our children, our relations, our servants, our friends, our neighbors, our worldly callings—each and all of these are fountains of care. Sicknesses, deaths, losses, disappointments, partings, separations, ingratitude, slander—all these are common things. We cannot get through life without them. Some day or other they find us out. The greater are our affections, the deeper are our afflictions; and the more we love, the more we have to weep.

And what is the best receipt for cheerfulness in such a world as this? How shall we get through this valley of tears with least pain? I know no better receipt than the habit of *taking everything to God in prayer*.

This is the plain advice that the Bible gives, both in the Old Testament and the New. What says the psalmist? "Call upon me in the day of trouble: I will deliver thee, and thou shalt glorify me" (Ps. 50:15). "Cast thy burden upon the Lord, and he shall sustain thee: he shall never suffer the righteous to be moved" (Ps. 55:22). What says the apostle Paul? "Be careful for nothing; but in every thing by prayer and supplication with thanksgiving let your requests be made known unto God. And the peace of God, which passeth all understanding, shall keep your hearts and minds through Christ Jesus" (Phil. 4:6, 7). What says the apostle James? "Is any among you afflicted? let him pray" (James 5:13).

This was the practice of all the saints whose history we have recorded in the Scriptures. This is what Jacob did, when he feared his brother Esau. This is what Moses did, when the people were ready to stone him in the wilderness. This is what Joshua did, when Israel was defeated before Ai. This is what David did, when he was in danger at Keliah. This is what Hezekiah did, when he received the letter from Sennacherib. This is what the church did, when Peter was put in prison. This is what Paul did, when he was cast into the dungeon at Philippi.

The only way to be really happy, in such a world as this, is to be ever casting all our cares on God. It is the trying to carry their own burdens which so often makes believers sad. If they will only tell their troubles to God He will enable them to bear them as easily as Samson did the gates of Gaza. If they are resolved to keep them to themselves they will find one day that the very grasshopper is a burden (Eccles. 12:5).

There is a friend ever waiting to help us, if we will only unbosom to Him our sorrow; a friend who pitied the poor, and sick, and sorrowful, when He was upon earth; a friend who knows the heart of a man, for He lived thirty-three years as a man amongst us; a friend who can weep with the weepers, for He was a man of sorrows and acquainted with grief; a friend who is able to help us, for there never was earthly pain He could not cure. That friend is Jesus Christ. The way to be happy is to be always opening our hearts to Him. Oh, that we were all like that poor Christian Negro, who only answered, when threatened and punished, "*I must tell the Lord.*"

Jesus can make those happy who trust Him and call on Him, whatever be their outward condition. He can give them peace of heart in a prison, contentment in the midst of poverty, comfort in the midst of bereavements, joy on the brink of the grave. There is a mighty fullness in Him for all His believing members—a fullness that is ready to be poured out on every one who will ask in prayer. Oh, that men would understand that happiness does not depend on outward circumstances, but on the state of the heart!

Prayer can lighten crosses for us however heavy. It can bring down to our side one who will help us to bear them. Prayer can open a door for us when our way seems hedged up. It can bring down one who will say, ''This is the way, walk in it.'' Prayer can let in a ray of hope, when all our earthly prospects seem darkened. It can bring down one who will say, ''I will never leave thee nor forsake thee.'' Prayer can obtain relief for us when those we love must be taken away, and the world feels empty. It can bring down one who can fill the gap in our hearts with Himself, and say to the waves within, ''Peace: be still!'' Oh, that men were not so like Hagar in the wilderness, blind to the well of living waters close beside them! (Gen. 21:19).

I want the readers of this paper to be really happy Christians. I am certain I cannot urge on them a more important duty than prayer.

And now it is high time for me to bring this paper to an end. I trust I have brought before my readers things that will be seriously considered. I heartily pray God that this consideration may be blessed to their souls.

(1) Let me speak a parting word *to those who do not pray*. I dare not suppose that all who read these pages will be praying people. If you are a prayerless person, suffer me to speak to you this day on God's behalf.

Prayerless friend, I can only warn you; but I do warn you most solemnly. I warn you that you are in a position of fearful danger. If you die in your present state you are a lost soul. You will only rise again to be eternally miserable. I warn you that of all professing Christians you are most utterly without excuse. There is not a single good reason that you can show for living without prayer.

It is useless to say you *know not how* to pray. Prayer is the simplest act in all religion, It is simply speaking to God. It needs neither learning, nor wisdom, nor bookknowledge to begin it. It needs nothing but heart and will. The weakest infant can cry when he is hungry. The poorest beggar can hold out his hand for an alms, and does not wait to find fine words. The most ignorant man will find something to say to God, if he has only a mind.

It is useless to say you have *no convenient place* to pray in. Any man can find a place private enough, if he is disposed. Our Lord prayed on a mountain; Peter on the housetop; Isaac in the field; Nathanael under the figtree; Jonah in the whales's belly. Any place may become a closet, an oratory, and a Bethal, and be to us the presence of God.

It is useless to say *you have no time*. There is plenty of time, if men will only employ it. Time may be short, but time is always long enough for prayer. Daniel had all the affairs of a kingdom on his hands, and yet he prayed three times a day. David was ruler over a mighty nation, and yet he says, "Evening, and morning, and at noon, will I pray" (Ps. 55:17). When time is really wanted, time can always be found.

It is useless to say you *cannot pray till you have faith and a new heart*, and that you must sit still and wait for them. This is to add sin to sin. It is bad enough to be unconverted and going to hell. It is even worse to say "I know it, but I will not cry for mercy." This is a kind of argument for which there is no warrant in Scripture. "Call ye upon the Lord," saith Isaiah, "while he is near" (Isa. 55:6). "Take with you words, and come unto the Lord," says Hosea (Hos. 14:2). "Repent and pray," says Peter to Simon Magus (Acts 8:22). If you want faith and a new heart, go and cry to the Lord for them. The very attempt to pray has often been the quickening of a dead soul. Alas, there is no devil so dangerous as a dumb devil.

Oh, prayerless man, who and what are you that you will not ask anything of God? Have you made a covenant with death and hell? Are you at peace with the worm and the fire? Have you no sins to be pardoned? Have you no fear of eternal torment? Have you no desire after heaven? Oh, that you would awake from your present folly! Oh, that you would consider your latter end! Oh, that you would arise and call upon God! Alas, there is a day coming when men shall pray loudly, "Lord, Lord, open to us," but all too late—when many shall cry to the rocks to fall on them, and the hills to cover them, who would never cry to God. In all affection I warn you. Beware lest this be the end of your soul. Salvation is very near you. Do not lose heaven for want of asking.

(2) Let me speak in the next place *to those who have real desires for salvation*, but know not what steps to take or where to begin. I cannot but hope that some readers may be in this state of mind, and if there be but one such I must offer him encouragement and advice.

In every journey there must be a first step. There must be a change from sitting still to moving forward. The journeyings of Israel from Egypt to Canaan were long and wearisome. Forty years passed away before they crossed Jordan. Yet there was someone who moved first when they marched from Rameses to Succoth. When does a man really take his first step in coming out from sin and the world? He does it in the day when he first prays with his heart.

In every building the first stone must be laid, and the first blow must be struck. The ark was 120 years in building. Yet there was a day when Noah laid his axe to the first tree he cut down to form it. The temple of Solomon was a glorious building. But there was a day when the first huge stone was laid at the foot of Mount Moriah. When does the building of the Spirit really begin to appear in a man's heart? It begins, so far as we can judge, when he first pours out his heart to God in prayer.

If any reader of this paper desires salvation, and wants to know what to do, I advise him to go this very day to the Lord Jesus Christ, in the first private place he can find, and entreat Him in prayer to save his soul.

Tell Him that you have heard that He receives sinners, and has said, "Him that cometh to me I will in no wise cast out" (John 6:37). Tell Him that you are a poor vile sinner, and that you come to Him on the faith of His own invitation. Tell Him you put yourself wholly and entirely in His hands; that you feel vile and helpless, and hopeless in yourself; and that except He saves you, you have no hope to be saved at all. Beseech Him to deliver you from the guilt, the power, and the consequences of sin. Beseech Him to pardon you and wash you in His own blood. Beseech Him to give you a new heart, and plant the Holy Spirit in your soul. Beseech Him to give you grace, and faith, and will, and power to be His disciple and servant from this day forever. Yes, go this very day, and tell these things to the Lord Jesus Christ, if you really are in earnest about your soul.

Tell Him in your own way and your own words. If a doctor came to see you when sick you could tell him where you felt pain. If your soul really feels its disease you can surely find something to tell Christ.

Doubt not His willingness to save you, because you are a sinner. It is Christ's office to save sinners. He says Himself, "I came not to call the righteous, but sinners to repentance" (Luke 5:32).

Wait not, because you feel unworthy. Wait for nothing; wait for nobody. Waiting comes from the devil.

Just as you are, go to Christ. The worse you are, the more need you have to apply to Him. You will never mend yourself by staying away.

Fear not because your prayer is stammering, your words feeble, and your language poor. Jesus can understand you. Just as a mother understands the first babblings of her infant, so does the blessed Savior understand sinners. He can read a sigh, and see a meaning in a groan.

Despair not, because you do not get an answer immediately. While you are speaking, Jesus is listening. If He delays an answer, it is only for wise reasons, and to try if you are in earnest. Pray on, and the answer will surely come. Though it tarry, wait for it: it will surely come at last.

If you have any desire to be saved, remember the advice I have given you this day. Act upon it honestly and heartily, and you shall be saved.

(3) Let me speak, lastly, *to those who do pray*. I trust that some who read this paper know well what prayer is, and have the Spirit of adoption. To all such I offer a few words of brotherly counsel and exhortation. The incense offered in the tabernacle was ordered to be made in a particular way. Not every kind of incense would do. Let us remember this, and be careful about the matter and manner of our prayers.

If I know anything of a Christian's heart, you to whom I now speak are often sick of your own prayers. You never enter into the apostle's words, "When I would do good, evil is present with me" (Rom. 7:21), so thoroughly as you sometimes do upon your knees. You can understand David's words, "I hate vain thoughts." You can sympathize with that poor converted Hottentot, who was overheard praying, "Lord, deliver me from all my enemies; and, above all, from that bad man myself!" There are few children of God who do not often find the season of prayer a season of conflict. The devil has special wrath against us when he sees us on our knees. Yet I believe that prayers which cost us no trouble should be regarded with great suspicion. I believe we are very poor judges of the goodness of our prayers, and that the prayer which pleases us *least* often pleases God *most*. Suffer me than, as a companion in the Christian warfare, to offer you a few words of exhortation. One thing, at least, we all feel—we must pray. We cannot give it up: we must go on.

(a) I commend, then, to your attention the importance of *reverence and humility* in prayer. Let us never forget what we are, and what a solemn thing it is to speak with God. Let us beware of rushing into His presence with carelessness and levity. Let us say to ourselves, "I am on holy ground. This is no other than the gate of heaven. If I do not mean what I say, I am trifling with God. If I regard iniquity in my heart, the Lord will not hear me." Let us keep in mind the words of Solomon: "Be not rash with thy mouth, and let not thine heart be hasty to utter any thing before God: for God is in heaven, and thou upon earth" (Eccles. 5:2). When Abraham spoke to God, he said, "I am dust and ashes." When Job spoke, he said, "I am vile" (Gen. 18:27; Job 45:4). Let us do likewise.

(b) I commend to you, in the next place, the importance of praying *spiritually*. I mean by this that we should labor always to have the direct help of the Spirit in our prayers, and beware above all things of formality. There is nothing so spiritual but that it may become a form, and this is specially true of private prayer. We may insensibly get into the habit of using the fittest possible words, and offering the most scriptural petitions; and yet we may do it all by rote, without feeling it, and walk daily round an old beaten path, like a horse in a mill. I

desire to touch this point with caution and delicacy. I
know that there are certain great things we daily want,
and that there is nothing necessarily formal in asking for
these things in the same words. The world, the devil,
and our hearts, are daily the same. Of necessity we must
daily go over old ground. But this I say—we must be
very careful on this point. If the skeleton and outline of
our prayers be by habit almost a form, let us strive that
the clothing and filling up of our prayers be as far as possible of the Spirit. As to praying out of a book, it is a
habit I cannot praise. If we can tell our doctors the state
of our bodies without a book, we ought to be able to tell
the state of our souls to God. I have no objection to a
man using crutches, when he is first recovering from a
broken limb. It is better to use crutches than not to walk
at all. But if I saw him all his life on crutches, I should
not think it matter for congratulation. I should like to
see him strong enough to throw his crutches away.

(c) I commend to you, in the next place, the importance of making prayer *a regular business of life*. I might
say something of the value of regular times in the day for
prayer. God is a God of order. The hours for morning
and evening sacrifice in the Jewish temple were not fixed
as they were without a meaning. Disorder is eminently
one of the fruits of sin. But I would not bring any under
bondage. This only I say, that it is essential to your soul's
health to make praying a part of the business of every
twenty-four hours in your life. Just as you allot time to
eating, sleeping, and business, so also allot time to
prayer. Choose your own hours and seasons. At the very
least, speak with God in the morning, before you speak
with the world; and speak with God at night, after you
have done with the world. But settle it down in your
minds that prayer is one of the great things of every day.
Do not drive it into a corner. Do not give it the scraps,

and leavings, and parings of your day. Whatever else you make a business of, make a business of prayer.

(d) I commend to you, in the next place, the importance of *perseverance* in prayer. Once having begun the habit, never give it up. Your heart will sometimes say, "We have had family prayers; what mighty harm if we leave private prayer undone?" Your body will sometimes say, "You are unwell, or sleepy, or weary; you need not pray." Your mind will sometimes say, "You have important business to attend to today; cut short your prayers." Look on all such suggestions as coming direct from the devil. They are all as good as saying, "Neglect your soul." I do not maintain that prayers should always be of the same length; but I do say, let no excuse make you give up prayer. It is not for nothing that Paul said, "Continue in prayer," and "Pray without ceasing" (Col. 4:2; I Thess. 5:7). He did not mean that men should be always on their knees, as as old sect, called the Euchitae, supposed. But he did mean that our prayers should be like the continual burnt offering—a thing steadily persevered in every day; that it should be like seed time and harvest, and summer and winter—a thing that should unceasingly come round at regular seasons; that it should be like the fire on the altar—not always consuming sacrifices, but never completely going out. Never forget that you may tie together morning and evening devotions by an endless chain of short ejaculatory prayers throughout the day. Even in company, or business, or in the very streets, you may be silently sending up little winged messengers to God, as Nehemiah did in the very presence of Artaxerxes (Neh. 2:4). And never think that time is wasted which is given to God. A nation does not become poorer because it loses one year of working days in seven by keeping the Sabbath. A Christian never finds he is a loser in the long run by persevering in prayer.

(e) I commend to you, in the next place, the importance of *earnestness* in prayer. It is not necessary that a man should shout, or scream, or be very loud, in order to prove that he is in earnest. But it is desirable that we should be hearty, and fervent, and warm, and ask as if we were really interested in what we were doing. It is the "effectual fervent" prayer that "availeth much," and not the cold, sleepy, lazy, listless one. This is the lesson that is taught us by the expressions used in Scripture about prayer. It is called, "crying, knocking, wrestling, laboring, striving." This is the lesson taught us by Scripture examples. Jacob is one. He said to the angel at Penuel, "I will not let thee go, except thou bless me" (Gen. 32:26). Daniel is another. Hear how he pleaded with God: "O Lord, hear; O Lord, forgive; O Lord, hearken and do; defer not, for thine own sake, O my God" (Dan. 9:19). Our Lord Jesus Christ is another. It is written of Him, "In the days of his flesh he offered up prayer and supplication, with strong crying and tears" (Heb. 5:7). Alas, how unlike is this to many of our supplications! How tame and lukewarm they seem by comparison! How truly might God say to many of us "You do not really want what you pray for!" Let us try to amend this fault. Let us knock loudly at the door of grace, like Mercy in "Pilgrim's Progress," as if we must perish unless heard. Let us settle it down in our minds, that cold prayers are a sacrifice without fire. Let us remember the story of Demosthenes, the great orator, when one came to him, and wanted him to plead his cause. He heard him without attention, while he told his story without earnestness. The man saw this, and cried out with anxiety that it was all true. "Ah!" said Demosthenes, "I believe you *now*."

(f) I commend to you, in the next place, the importance of *praying with faith*. We should endeavor to believe that our prayers are always heard, and that if we ask

things according to God's will, we shall always be answered. This is the plain command of our Lord Jesus Christ: "What things soever ye desire, when ye pray, believe that ye receive them, and ye shall have them" (Mark 11:24). Faith is to prayer what the feather is to the arrow: without it prayer will not hit the mark. We should cultivate the habit of pleading promises in our prayers. We should take with us some promise, and say, "Lord, here is thine own word pledged. Do for us as thou hast said" (II Sam. 7:25). This was the habit of Jacob, and Moses, and David. The 119th Psalm is full of things asked, "according to thy word." Above all, we should cultivate the habit of expecting answers to our prayers. We should do like the merchant who sends his ships to sea. We should not be satisfied unless we see some return. Alas, there are few points on which Christians come short so much as this. The church at Jerusalem made prayer without ceasing for Peter in prison; but when the prayer was answered, they would hardly believe it (Acts 12:15). It is a solemn saying of old Traill's, "There is no surer mark of trifling in prayer, than when men are careless what they get by prayer."

(g) I commend to you, in the next place, the importance of *boldness* in prayer. There is an unseemly familiarity in some men's prayers, which I cannot praise. But there is such a thing as a holy boldness, which is exceedingly to be desired. I mean such boldness as that of Moses, when he pleads with God not to destroy Israel: "Wherefore," says he, "should the Egyptians speak, and say, For mischief did he bring them out, to slay them in the mountains? Turn from thy fierce anger" (Exod. 32:12). I mean such boldness as that of Joshua, when the children of Israel were defeated before Ai: "What," says he, "wilt thou do unto thy great name?" (Josh. 7:9). This is the boldness for which Luther was remarkable. One who heard him praying said, "What a spirit, what a confidence was in his very expressions! With such a reverence he sued, as one begging of God, and yet with such hope and assurance, as if he spake with a loving father or friend." This is the boldness which distinguished Bruce, a great Scotch divine of the seventeenth century. His prayers were said to be "like bolts shot up into heaven." Here also I fear we sadly come short. We do not sufficiently realize the believer's privileges. We do not plead as often as we might, "Lord, are we not thine own people? Is it not for thy glory that we should be sanctified? Is it not for thine honor that the gospel should increase?"

(h) I commend to you, in the next place, the importance of *fullness* in prayer. I do not forget that our Lord warns us against the example of the Pharisees, who for pretense made long prayers, and commands us, when we pray, not to use vain repetitions. But I cannot forget, on the other hand, that He has given His own sanction to large and long devotions, by continuing all night in prayer to God. At all events we are not likely in this day to err on the side of praying *too much*. Might it not rather be feared that many believers in this generation pray *too little*? Is not the actual amount of time that many Christians give to prayer in the aggregate very small? I am afraid these questions cannot be answered satisfactorily. I am afraid the private devotions of many are most painfully scanty and limited—just enough to prove they are alive, and no more. They really seem to want little from God. They seem to have little to confess, little to ask for, and little to thank Him for. Alas, this is altogether wrong! Nothing is more common than to hear believers complaining that they do not get on. They tell us that they do not grow in grace, as they could desire. It is not rather to be suspected that many have quite as much grace as they ask for? Is it not the true account of many, that they have little, because they ask little? The cause of their weakness is to be found in their own stunted, dwarfish, clipped, contracted, hurried, little, narrow, diminutive prayers. *They have not because they ask not*. Oh, reader, we are not straitened in Christ, but in ourselves. The Lord says, ''Open thy mouth wide, and I will fill it.'' But we are like the king of Israel who smote on the ground thrice and stayed, when he ought to have smitten five or six times (Ps. 81:10; II Kings 13:18, 19).

(i) I commend you, in the next place, the importance of *particularity* in prayer. We ought not to be content with great general petitions. We ought to specify our wants before the throne of grace. It should not be enough to confess we are sinners. We should name the sins of which our conscience tells us we are most guilty. It should not be enough to ask for holiness. We should name the graces in which we feel most deficient. It should not be enough to tell the Lord we are in trouble. We should describe our troubles and all its peculiarities. This is what Jacob did, when he feared his brother Esau. He tells God exactly what it is that he fears (Gen. 32:11). This is what Eliezer did, when he sought a wife for his master's son. He spreads before God precisely what he wants (Gen. 24:12-14). This is what Paul did, when he had a thorn in the flesh. He besought the Lord (II Cor. 12:8). This is true faith and confidence. We should believe that nothing is too small to be named before God. What should we think of the patient who told his doctor he was ill, but never went into particulars? What should we think of the wife who told her husband she was unhappy, but did not specify the cause? What should we think of the child who told his father he was in trouble, but nothing more? Let us never forget that Christ is the true bridegroom of the soul, the true physician of the heart, the real father of all His people. Let us show that we feel this, by being unreserved in our communications with Him. Let us hide no secrets from Him. Let us tell Him all our hearts.

(*j*) I commend to you, in the next place, the importance of *intercession* in our prayers. We are all selfish by nature and our selfishness is very apt to stick to us, even when we are converted. There is a tendency in us to think only of our own souls, our own spiritual conflict, our own progress in religion, and to forget others. Against this tendency we have all need to watch and strive, and not least in our prayers. We should study to be of a public spirit. We should stir ourselves up to name other names beside our own before the throne of grace. We should try to bear in our hearts the whole world—the heathen, the Jews, the Roman Catholics, the body of true believers, the professing Protestant churches, the country in which we live, the congregation to which we belong, the household in which we sojourn, the friends and relations we are connected with. For each and all of these we should plead. This is the highest charity. He loves me best who loves me in his prayers. This is for our soul's health. It enlarges our sympathies and expands our hearts. This is for the benefit of the church. The wheels of all machinery for extending the gospel are oiled by prayer. They do as much for the Lord's cause who intercede like Moses on the mount, as they do who fight like Joshua in the thick of the battle. This is to be like Christ. He bears the names of His people on His breast and shoulders as their High Priest before the Father. Oh, the privilege of being like Jesus! This is to be a true helper to ministers. If I must needs choose a congregation, give me a people that prays.

(*k*) I commend to you, in the next place, the importance of *thankfulness* in prayer. I know well that asking God is one thing, and praising God is another. But I see so close a connection between prayer and praise in the Bible, that I dare not call that true prayer in which thankfulness has no part. It is not for nothing that Paul says, ''By prayer and supplication with thanksgiving let your requests be made known unto God'' (Phil. 4:6). ''Continue in prayer, and watch in the same with thanksgiving'' (Col. 4:2). It is of mercy that we are not in hell. It is of mercy that we have the hope of heaven. It is of mercy that we live in a land of spiritual light. It is of mercy that we have been called by the Spirit, and not left to reap the fruit of our own ways. It is of mercy that we still live, and have opportunities of glorifying God actively or passively. Surely, these thoughts should crowd on our minds whenever we speak with God. Surely, we should never open our lips in prayer without blessing God for that free grace by which we live, and for that loving-kindness which endureth forever. Never was there an eminent saint who was not full of thankfulness. St. Paul hardly ever writes an epistle without beginning with thankfulness. Men like Whitefield in the last century, and Bickersteth, and Marsh, and Haldane Stewart, in our own time, were ever running over with thankfulness. Oh, if we would be bright and shining lights in our day, we must cherish a spirit of praise! And above all, let our prayers be thankful prayers.

(l) I commend to you, in the last place, the importance of *watchfulness over your prayers*. Prayer is that point of all others in religion at which you must be on your guard. Here it is that true religion begins: here it flourishes, and here it decays. Tell me what a man's prayers are, and I will soon tell you the state of his soul. Prayer is the spiritual pulse: by this the spiritual health may always be tested. Prayer is the spiritual weatherglass: by this we may always know whether it is fair or foul with our hearts. Oh, let us keep an eye continually upon our private devotions! Here is the pith, and marrow, and backbone of our practical Christianity. Sermons, and books, and tracts, and committee meetings, and the company of good men, are all good in their way; but they will never make up for the neglect of private prayer. Mark well the places, and society, and companions, that unhinge your hearts for communion with God, and make your prayers drive heavily. *There be on your guard.* Observe narrowly what friends and what employments leave your soul in the most spiritual frame, and most ready to speak with God. *To these cleave and stick fast.* If you will only take care of your prayers, I will engage that nothing shall go very wrong with your soul.

I offer these points for private consideration. I do it in all humility. I know no one who needs to be reminded of them more than I do myself. But I believe them to be God's own truth, and I should like myself and all I love to feel them more.

I want the times we live in to be praying times. I want the Christians of our day to be praying Christians. I want the church of our age to be a praying church. My heart's desire and prayer in sending forth this paper is to promote a spirit of prayerfulness. I want those who never prayed yet, to rise and call upon God; and I want those who do pray, to improve their prayers every year, and to see that they are not getting slack, and praying amiss.

6
Bible Reading

"Search the scriptures."—John 5:39
"How readest thou?"—Luke 10:26

Next to praying there is nothing so important in practical religion as Bible reading. God has mercifully given us a book which is "able to make us wise unto salvation through faith which is in Christ Jesus" (II Tim. 3:15). By reading that book we may learn what to believe, what to be, and what to do; how to live with comfort, and how to die in peace. Happy is that man who possesses a Bible! Happier still is he who reads it! Happiest of all is he who not only reads it, but obeys it, and makes it the rule of his faith and practice!

Nevertheless it is a sorrowful fact that man has an unhappy skill in abusing God's gifts. His privileges, and power, and faculties, are all ingeniously perverted to other ends than those for which they were bestowed. His speech, his imagination, his intellect, his strength, his time, his influence, his money—instead of being used as instruments for glorifying his Maker—are generally wasted, or employed for his own selfish ends. And just as man naturally makes a bad use of his other mercies, so he does of the written Word. One sweeping charge may be brought against the whole of Christendom, and that charge is neglect and abuse of the Bible.

To prove this charge we have no need to look abroad: the proof lies at our own doors. I have no doubt that there are more Bibles in Great Britain at this moment than there ever were since the world began. There is more Bible buying and Bible selling, more Bible printing and Bible distributing, than ever was since England was a nation. We see Bibles in every bookseller's shop, Bibles of every size, price, and style, Bibles great, and Bibles small, Bibles for the rich, and Bibles for the poor. There are Bibles in almost every house in the land. But all this time I fear we are in danger of forgetting, that to *have* the Bible is one thing, and to *read* it quite another.

This neglected book is the subject about which I address the readers of this paper today. Surely it is no light matter *what you are doing with the Bible*. Surely, when the plague is abroad, you should search and see whether the plague-spot is on you. Give me your attention while I supply you with a few plain reasons why every one who cares for his soul ought to value the Bible highly, to study it regularly, and to make himself thoroughly acquainted with its contents.

I. In the first place, *there is no book in existence written in such a manner as the Bible*.

The Bible was "given by inspiration of God" (II Tim.3:16). In this respect it is utterly unlike all other writings. God taught the writers of it what to say. God put into their minds thoughts and ideas. God guided their pens in setting down those thoughts and ideas. When you read it, you are not reading the self-taught compositions of poor imperfect men like yourself, but the words of the eternal God. When you hear it, you are not listening to the erring opinions of short-lived mortals, but to the unchanging mind of the King of kings. The men who were employed to indite the Bible, spoke not of themselves. They "spake as they were moved by the Holy Ghost" (II Peter 1:21). All other books in the world, however good and useful in their way, are more or less defective. The more you look at them the more you see their defects and blemishes. The Bible alone is absolutely perfect. From beginning to end it is "the Word of God."

I shall not waste time by attempting any long and labored proof of this. I say boldly, that the book itself is the best witness of it own inspiration. It is utterly inexplicable and uaccountable in any other point of view. It is the greatest standing miracle in the world. He that dares to say the Bible is not inspired, let him give a reasonable account of it, if he can. Let him explain the peculiar nature and character of the book in a way that will satisfy any man of common sense. The burden of proof seems to my mind to lie on him.

It proves nothing against inspiration, as some have asserted, that the writers of the Bible have each a different style. Isaiah does not write like Jeremiah, and Paul does not write like John. This is perfectly true, and yet the works of these men are not a whit less equally inspired. The waters of the sea have many different shades. In one place they look blue, and in another green. And yet the difference is owing to the depth or shallowness of the part we see, or to the nature of the bottom. The water in every case is the same salt sea. The breath of a man may produce different sounds, according to the character of the instrument on which he plays. The flute, the pipe, and the trumpet, have each their peculiar note. And yet the breath that calls forth the notes, is in each case one and the same. The light of the planets we see in heaven is very various. Mars, and

Saturn, and Jupiter, have each a peculiar color. And yet we know that the light of the sun, which each planet reflects, is in each case one and the same. Just in the same way the books of the Old and New Testaments are all inspired truth, and yet the aspect of that truth varies according to the mind through which the Holy Ghost makes it flow. The handwriting and style of the writers differ enough to prove that each had a distinct individual being; but the divine guide who dictates and directs the whole is always one. All is alike inspired. Every chapter, and verse, and word, is from God.

Oh, that men who are troubled with doubts, and questionings, and sceptical thoughts about inspiration, would calmly examine the Bible for themselves! Oh, that they would act on the advice which was the first step to Augustine's conversion, "Take it up and read it!— take it up and read it!" How many Gordian knots this course of action would cut! How many difficulties and objections would vanish away at once like mist before the rising sun! How many would soon confess, "The finger of God is here! God is in this book, and I knew it not."

This is the book about which I address the readers of this paper. Surely it is no light matter *what you are doing with this book*. It is no light thing that God should have caused this book to be "written for your learning," and that you should have before you "the oracles of God" (Rom. 3:2; 15:4). I charge you, I summon you to give an honest answer to my question. What art thou doing with the Bible? Dost thou read it at all? HOW READEST THOU?

II. In the second place, *there is no knowledge absolutely needful to a man's salvation, except a knowledge of the things which are to be found in the Bible.*

We live in days when the words of Daniel are fulfilled before our eyes: "Many run to and fro, and knowledge is increased" (Dan. 12:4). Schools are multiplying on every side. New colleges are set up. Old universities are reformed and improved. New books are continually coming forth. More is being taught, more is being learned, more is being read, than there ever was since the world began. It is all well. I rejoice at it. An ignorant population is a perilous and expensive burden to any nation. It is a ready prey to the first Absalom, Catiline, or Wat Tyler, or Jack Cade, who may arise to entice it to do evil. But this I say—we must never forget that all the education a man's head can receive, will not save his soul from hell, unless he knows the truths of the Bible.

A man *may have prodigious learning, and yet never be saved*. He may be master of half the languages spoken round the globe. He may be acquainted with the highest and deepest things in heaven and earth. He may have read books till he is like a walking encyclopedia. He may be familiar with the stars of heaven, the birds of the air, the beasts of the earth, and the fishes of the sea. He may be able, like Solomon, to "speak of trees, from the cedar of Lebanon to the hyssop that grows on the wall, of beasts also, and fowls, and creeping things, and fishes" (I Kings 4:33). He may be able to discourse of all the secrets of fire, air, earth, and water. And yet, if he dies ignorant of Bible truths, he dies a miserable man! Chemistry never silenced a guilty conscience. Mathematics never healed a broken heart. All the sciences in the world never smoothed down a dying pillow. No earthly philosophy ever supplied hope in death. No natural theology ever gave peace in the prospect of meeting a holy God. All these things are of the earth, earthy, and can never raise a man above the earth's level. They may enable a man to strut and fret his little season here below with a more dignified gait than his fellow mortals, but they can never give him wings, and enable him to soar towards heaven. He that has the largest share of them, will find at length that without Bible knowledge he has got no lasting possession. Death will make an end of all his attainments, and after death they will do him no good at all.

A man *may be a very ignorant man, and yet be saved*. He may be unable to read a word, or write a letter. He may know nothing of geography beyond the bounds of his own parish, and be utterly unable to say which is nearest to England, Paris or New York. He may know nothing of arithmetic, and not see any difference between a million and a thousand. He may know nothing of history, not even of his own land, and be quite ignorant whether his country owes most to Semiramis, Boadicea, or Queen Elizabeth. He may know nothing of the affairs of his own times, and be incapable of telling you whether the Chancellor of the Exchequer, or the Commander-in-Chief, or the Archbishop of Canterbury is managing the national finances. He may know nothing of science, and its discoveries—and whether Julius Caesar won his victories with gunpowder, or the apostles had a printing press, or the sun goes round the earth, may be matters about which he has not an idea. And yet if that very man has heard Bible truth with his ears, and believed it with his heart, he knows enough to save his soul. He will be found at last with Lazarus in Abraham's bosom, while his scientific fellow-creature, who has died unconverted, is lost forever.

There is much to talk in these days about science and "useful knowledge." But, after all, a knowledge of the Bible is the one knowledge that is needful and eternally useful. A man may get to heaven without money, learning, health, or friends—but without Bible knowledge he will never get there at all. A man may have the mightiest of minds, and a memory stored with all that mighty mind can grasp—and yet, if he does not know the things of the Bible, he will make shipwreck of his soul forever. Woe! woe! woe to the man who dies in ignorance of the Bible!

This is the book about which I am addressing the readers of these pages today. It is no light matter *what you do with such a book*. It concerns the life of your soul. I summon you, I charge you to give an honest answer to my question. What are you doing with the Bible? Do you read it? HOW READEST THOU?

III. In the third place, *no book in existence contains such important matter as the Bible*.

The time would fail me if I were to enter fully into all the great things which are to be found in the Bible, and only in the Bible. It is not by any sketch or outline that the treasures of the Bible can be displayed. It would be easy to fill this volume with a list of the peculiar truths it reveals, and yet the half of its riches would be left untold.

How glorious and soul-satisfying is the description it gives us of God's plan of salvation, and the way by which our sins can be forgiven! The coming into the world of Jesus Christ, the God-man, to save sinners; the atonement He has made by suffering in our stead, the just for the unjust; the complete payment He has made for our sins by His own blood; the justification of every sinner who simply believes on Jesus; the readiness of Father, Son, and Holy Ghost, to receive, pardon, and save to the uttermost—how unspeakably grand and cheering are all these truths! We should know nothing of them without the Bible.

How comforting is the account it gives us of the great mediator of the New Testament—the man Christ Jesus! Four times over His picture is graciously drawn before our eyes. Four separate witnesses tell us of His miracles and His ministry, His sayings and His doings, His life and His death, His power and His love, His kindness and His patience, His ways, His words, His works, His thoughts, His heart. Blessed be God, there is one thing in the Bible which the most prejudiced reader can hardly fail to understand, and that is the character of Jesus Christ!

How encouraging are the examples the Bible gives us of good people! It tells us of many who were of like passions with ourselves—men and women who had cares, crosses, families, temptations, afflictions, diseases, like ourselves—and yet "by faith and patience inherited the promises," and got safe home (Heb. 6:12). It keeps back nothing in the history of these people. Their mistakes, their infirmities, their conflicts, their experience, their prayers, their praises, their useful lives, their happy deaths—all are fully recorded. And it tells us the God and Savior of these men and women still waits to be gracious, and is altogether unchanged.

How instructive are the examples the Bible gives us of bad people! It tells us of men and women who had light, and knowledge, and opportunities, like ourselves, and yet hardened their hearts, loved the world, clung to their sins, would have their own way, despised reproof, and ruined their own souls forever. And it warns us that the God who punished Pharaoh, and Saul, and Ahab, and Jezebel, and Judas, and Ananias and Sapphira, is a God who never alters, and that there is a hell.

How precious are the promises which the Bible contains for the use of those who love God! There is hardly any possible emergency or condition for which it has not some "word in season." And it tells men that God loves to be put in remembrance of these promises, and that if He has said He will do a thing, His promise shall certainly be performed.

How blessed are the hopes which the Bible holds out to the believer in Christ Jesus! Peace in the hour of death, rest and happiness on the other side of the grave, a glorious body in the morning of the resurrection, a full and triumphant acquittal in the day of judgment, an everlasting reward in the kingdom of Christ, a joyful meeting with the Lord's people in the day of gathering together—these, these are the future prospects of every true Christian. They are all written in the book—in the book which is all true.

How striking is the light which the Bible throws on the character of man! It teaches us what men may be expected to be and do in every position and station of life. It gives us the deepest insight into the secret springs and motives of human actions, and the ordinary course of events under the control of human agents. It is the true "discerner of the thoughts and intents of the heart" (Heb. 4:12). How deep is the wisdom contained in the books of Proverbs and Ecclesiastes! I can well understand an old divine saying, "Give me a candle and a Bible, and shut me up in a dark dungeon, and I will tell you all that the whole world is doing."

All these are things which men could find nowhere except in the Bible. We have probably not the least idea how little we should know about these things if we had not the Bible. We hardly know the value of the air we breathe, and the sun which shines on us, because we have never known what it is to be without them. We do not value the truths on which I have been just now dwelling, because we do not realize the darkness of men to whom these truths have not been revealed. Surely no tongue can fully tell the value of the treasures this one volume contains. Well might old John Newton say that some books were *copper* books in his estimation, some were *silver*, and some few were *gold*; but the Bible alone was like a book all made up of *bank notes*.

This is the book about which I address the reader of this paper this day. Surely it is no light matter *what you are doing with the Bible*. It is no light matter in what way you are using this treasure. I charge you, I summon you to give an honest answer to my question. What art thou doing with the Bible? Dost thou read it? HOW READEST THOU?

IV. In the fourth place, *no book in existence has produced such wonderful effects on mankind at large as the Bible*.

(a) This is the book whose doctrines turned the world upside down in the days of the apostles.

Eighteen centuries have now passed away since God sent forth a few Jews from a remote corner of the earth, to do a work which according to man's judgment must have seemed impossible. He sent them forth at a time when the whole world was full of superstition, cruelty, lust, and sin. He sent them forth to proclaim that the established religions of the earth were false and useless, and must be forsaken. He sent them forth to persuade men to give up old habits and customs, and to live different lives. He sent them forth to do battle with the most groveling idolatry, with the vilest and most disgusting immorality, with vested interests, with old associations, with a bigoted priesthood, with sneering philosophers, with an ignorant population, with bloody-minded emperors, with the whole influence of Rome. Never was there an enterprise to all appearance more quixotic, and less likely to succeed!

And how did He arm them for this battle? He gave them no carnal weapons. He gave them no worldly power to compel assent, and no worldly riches to bribe belief. He simply put the Holy Ghost into their hearts, and the Scriptures into their hands. He simply bade them to expound and explain, to enforce and to publish the doctrines of the Bible. The preacher of Christianity in the first century was not a man with a sword and an army, to frighten people, like Mahomet, or a man with a license to be sensual, to allure people, like the priests of the shameful idols of Hindostan. No! he was nothing more than one holy man with one holy book.

And how did these men of one book prosper? In a few generations they entirely changed the face of society by the doctrines of the Bible. They emptied the temples of the heathen gods. They famished idolatry, or left it high and dry like a stranded ship. They brought into the world a higher tone of morality between man and man. They raised the character and position of woman. They altered the standard of purity and decency. They put an end to many cruel and bloody customs, such as the gladiatorial fights. There is no stopping the change. Persecution and opposition were useless. One victory after another was won. One bad thing after another melted away. Whether men liked it or not, they were insensibly affected by the movement of the new religion, and drawn within the whirlpool of its power. The earth shook, and their rotten refuges fell to the ground. The flood rose, and they found themselves obliged to rise with it. The tree of Christianity swelled and grew, and the chains they had cast round it to arrest its growth, snapped like tow. And all this was done by the doctrines of the Bible! Talk of victories indeed! What are the victories of Alexander, and Caesar, and Marlborough, and Napoleon, and Wellington, compared with those I have just mentioned? For extent, for completeness, for results, for permanence, there are no victories like the victories of the Bible.

(b) This is the book which turned Europe upside down in the days of the glorious Protestant Reformation.

No man can read the history of Christendom as it was five hundred years ago, and not see that darkness covered the whole professing church of Christ, even a darkness that might be felt. So great was the change which had come over Christianity, that if an apostle had risen from the dead he would not have recognized it, and would have thought that heathenism had revived again. The doctrines of the gospel lay buried under a dense mass of human traditions. Penances, and pilgrimages, and indulgences, relic-worship, and image-worship, and saint-worship, and worship of the Virgin Mary, formed the sum and substance of most people's religion. The church was made an idol. The priests and ministers of the church usurped the place of Christ. And by what means was all this miserable darkness cleared away? By none so much as by bringing forth once more the Bible.

It was not merely the preaching of Luther and his friends, which established Protestantism in Germany. The grand lever which overthrew the pope's power in that country, was Luther's translation of the Bible into the German tongue. It was not merely the writings of Cranmer and the English Reformers which cast down popery in England. The seeds of the work thus carried forward were first sown by Wycliffe's translation of the Bible many years before. It was not merely the quarrel of

Henry VIII and the pope of Rome, which loosened the pope's hold on English minds. It was the royal permission to have the Bible translated and set up in churches, so that every one who liked might read it. Yes, it was the reading and circulation of Scripture which mainly established the cause of Protestantism in England, in Germany, and Switzerland. Without it the people would probably have returned to their former bondage when the first Reformers died. But by the reading of the Bible the public mind became gradually leavened with the principles of true religion. Men's eyes became thoroughly open. Their spiritual understandings became thoroughly enlarged. The abominations of popery became distinctly visible. The excellence of the pure gospel became a rooted idea in their hearts. It was then in vain for popes to thunder forth excommunications. It was useless for kings and queens to attempt to stop the course of Protestantism by fire and sword. It was all too late. The people knew too much. They had seen the light. They had heard the joyful sound. They had tasted the truth. The sun had risen on their minds. The scales had fallen from their eyes. The Bible had done its appointed work within them, and that work was not to be overthrown. The people would not return to Egypt. The clock would not be put back again. A mental and moral revolution had been effected, and mainly effected by God's Word. Those are the true revolutions which the Bible effects. What are all the revolutions recorded by Vertot, what are all the revolutions which France and England have gone through, compared to these? No revolutions are so bloodless, none so satisfactory, none so rich in lasting results, as the revolutions accomplished by the Bible!

This is the book on which the well-being of nations has always hinged, and with which the best interests of every nation in Christendom at this moment are inseparably bound up. Just in proportion as the Bible is honored or not, light or darkness, morality or immorality, true religion or superstition, liberty or despotism, good laws or bad, will be found in a land. Come with me and open the pages of history, and you will read the proofs in time past. Read it in the history of Israel under the Kings. How great was the wickedness that then prevailed! But who can wonder? The law of the Lord had been completely lost sight of, and was found in the days of Josiah thrown aside in a corner of the temple (II Kings 22:8). Read it in the history of the Jews in our Lord Jesus Christ's time. How awful the picture of scribes and Pharisees, and their religion! But who can wonder? The Scripture was "made of none effect by man's traditions" (Matt. 15:6). Read it in the history of the church of Christ in the middle ages. What can be worse than the accounts we have of its ignorance and superstition? But who can wonder? The times might well be dark, when men had not the light of the Bible.

This is the book to which the civilized world is indebted for many of its best and most praiseworthy institutions. Few probably are aware how many are the good things that men have adopted for the public benefit, of which the origin may be clearly traced up to the Bible. It has left lasting marks wherever it has been received. From the Bible are drawn many of the best laws by which society is kept in order. From the Bible has been obtained the standard of morality about truth, honesty, and the relations of man and wife, which prevails among Christian nations, and which—however feebly respected in many cases—makes so great a difference between Christians and heathen. To the Bible we are indebted for that most merciful provision for the poor man, the Sabbath day. To the influence of the Bible we owe nearly every humane and charitable institution in existence. The sick, the poor, the aged, the orphan, the lunatic, the idiot, the blind, were seldom or never thought of before the Bible leavened the world. You may search in vain for any record of institutions for their aid in the histories of Athens or of Rome. Alas, there are many who sneer at the Bible, and say the world would get on well enough without it, who little think how great are their own obligations to the Bible. Little does the infidel workman think, as he lies sick in some of our great hospitals, that he owes all his present comforts to the very book he affects to despise. Had it not been for the Bible, he might have died in misery, uncared for, unnoticed and alone. Verily the world we live in is fearfully unconscious of its debts. The last day alone, I believe, will tell the full amount of benefit conferred upon it by the Bible.

This wonderful book is the subject about which I address the reader of this paper this day. Surely it is no light matter *what you are doing with the Bible*. The swords of conquering generals, the ship in which Nelson led the fleets of England to victory, the hydraulic press which raised the tubular bridge at the Menai—each and all of these are objects of interest as instruments of mighty power. The book I speak of this day is an instrument a thousandfold mightier still. Surely it is no light matter whether you are paying it the attention it deserves. I charge you, I summon you to give me an honest answer this day—What are thou doing with the Bible? Dost thou read it? HOW READEST THOU?

V. In the fifth place, *no book in existence can do so much for every one who reads it rightly as the Bible*.

The Bible does not profess to teach the wisdom of this world. It was not written to explain geology or astronomy. It will neither instruct you in mathematics, nor in natural philosophy. It will not make you a doctor, or a lawyer, or an engineer.

But there is another world to be thought of, beside that world in which man now lives. There are other ends for which man was created, beside making money and working. There are other interests which he is meant to attend to, beside those of his body, and those interests are the interests of his soul. It is the interests of the immortal soul which the Bible is especially able to promote. If you would know law, you may study Blackstone or Sugden. If you would know astronomy or geology, you may study Herschel and Lyell. But if you would know how to have your soul saved, you must study the written Word of God.

The Bible is *"able to make a man wise unto salvation through faith which is in Christ Jesus"* (II Tim. 3:15). It can show you the way which leads to heaven. It can teach you everything you need to know, point out everything you need to believe, and explain everything you need to do. It can show you what you are—*a sinner*. It can show you what God is—perfectly *holy*. It can show you the great giver of pardon, peace, and grace—*Jesus Christ*. I have read of an Englishman who visited Scotland in the days of Blair, Rutherford, and Dickson, three famous preachers, and heard all three in succession. He said that the first showed him the majesty of God, the second showed him the beauty of Christ, and the third showed him all his heart. It is the glory and beauty of the Bible that it is always teaching these three things more or less, from the first chapter of it to the last.

The Bible applied to the heart by the Holy Ghost, is *the grand instrument by which souls are first converted to God*. That mighty change is generally begun by some text or doctrine of the Word, brought home to a man's conscience. In this way the Bible has worked moral miracles by thousands. It has made drunkards become sober, unchaste people become pure, thieves become honest, and violent-tempered people become meek. It has wholly altered the course of men's lives. It has caused their old things to pass away, and made all their ways new. It has taught worldly people to seek first the kingdom of God. It has taught lovers of pleasure to become lovers of God. It has taught the stream of men's affections to run upwards instead of running downwards. It has made men think of heaven, instead of always thinking of earth, and live by faith, instead of living by sight. All this it has done in every part of the world. All this it is doing still. What are the Romish miracles which weak men believe, compared to all this, even if they were true? Those are the truly great miracles which are yearly worked by the Word.

The Bible applied to the heart by the Holy Ghost, is *the chief means by which men are built up and established in the faith,* after their conversion. It is able to cleanse them, to sanctify them, to instruct them in righteousness, and to furnish them thoroughly for all good works (Ps. 119:9; John 17:17; II Tim. 3:16, 17). The Spirit ordinarily does these things by the written Word; sometimes by the Word read, and sometimes by the Word preached, but seldom, if ever, without the Word. The Bible can show a believer how to walk in this world so as to please God. It can teach him how to glorify Christ in all the relations of life, and can make him a good master, servant, subject, husband, father, or son. It can enable him to bear afflictions and privations without murmuring, and say, "It is well." It can enable him to look down into the grave, and say, "I fear no evil" (Ps. 23:4). It can enable him to think on judgment and eternity, and not feel afraid. It can enable him to bear persecution without flinching, and to give up liberty and life rather than deny Christ's truth. Is he drowsy in soul? It can awaken him. Is he mourning? It can comfort him. Is he erring? It can restore him. Is he weak? It can make him strong. Is he in company? It can keep him from evil. Is he alone? It can talk with him. (Prov. 6:22). All this the Bible can do for all believers, for the least as well as the greatest, for the richest as well as the poorest. It has done it for thousands already, and is doing it for thousands every day.

The man who has the Bible, and the Holy Spirit in his heart, has everything which is absolutely needful to make him spiritually wise. He needs no priest to break the bread of life for him. He needs no ancient traditions, no writings of the Fathers, no voice of the church, to guide him into all truth. He has the well of truth open before him, and what can he want more? Yes, though he be shut up alone in a prison, or cast on a desert island, though he never see a church, or minister, or sacrament again—if he has but the Bible, he has got the infallible guide, and wants no other. If he has but the will to read that Bible rightly, it will certainly teach him the road that leads to heaven. It is here alone that infallibility resides. It is not in the church. It is not in the councils. It is not in ministers. It is only in the written Word.

(a) I know well that many say they have found no saving power in the Bible. They tell us they have tried to read it, and have learned nothing from it. They can see in it nothing but hard and deep things. They ask us what we mean by talking of its power.

I answer, that the Bible no doubt contains hard things, or else it would not be the book of God. It contains things hard to comprehend, but only hard because we have not grasp of mind to comprehend them. It contains things above our reasoning powers, but nothing that might not be explained if the eyes of our understanding were not feeble and dim. But is not an acknowledgment of our own ignorance the very cornerstone and foundation of all knowledge? Must not many things be taken for granted in the beginning of every science, before we can proceed one step towards acquaintance with it? Do we not require our children to learn many things of which they cannot see the meaning at first? And ought we not then to expect to find "deep things" when we begin studying the Word of God, and yet to believe that if we persevere in reading it the meaning of many of them will one day be made clear? No doubt we ought so to expect, and so to believe. We must read with humility. We must take much on trust. We must believe that what we know not now, we shall know hereafter—some part in this world, and all in the world to come.

But I ask that man who has given up reading the Bible because it contains hard things, whether he did not find many things in it easy and plain? I put it to his conscience whether he did not see great landmarks and principles in it all the way through? I ask him whether the things needful to salvation did not stand out boldly before his eyes, like the lighthouses on English headlands from the land's end to the mouth of the Thames. What should we think of the captain of a steamer who brought up at night in the entrance of the Channel, on the plea that he did not know every parish, and village, and creek, along the British coast? Should we not think him a lazy coward, when the lights on the Lizard, and Eddystone, and the Start, and Portland, and St. Catherine's, and Beachy Head, and Dungeness, and the Forelands, were shining forth like so many lamps, to guide him up to the river? Should we not say, "Why did you not steer by the great leading lights?" And what ought we to say to the man who gives up reading the Bible because it contains hard things, when his own state, and the path to heaven, and the way to serve God, are all written down clearly and unmistakably, as with a sunbeam? Surely we ought to tell that man that his objections are no better than lazy excuses, and do not deserve to be heard.

(b) I know well that many raise the objection, that thousands read the Bible and are not a whit the better for their reading. And they ask us, when this is the case, what becomes of the Bible's boasted power?

I answer, that the reason why so many read the Bible without benefit is plain and simple—they do not read it in the right way. There is generally a right way and a wrong way of doing everything in the world; and just as it is with other things, so it is in the matter of reading the Bible. The Bible is not so entirely different from all other books as to make it of no importance in what spirit and manner you read it. It does not do good, as a matter of course, by merely running our eyes over the print, any more than the sacraments do good by mere virtue of our receiving them. It does not ordinarily do good, unless it is read with humility and earnest prayer. The best steam engine that was ever built is useless if a man does not know how to work it. The best sundial that was ever constructed will not tell its owner the time of day if he is so ignorant as to put it up in the shade. Just as it is with that steam engine, and that sundial, so it is with the Bible. When men read it without profit, *the fault is not in the book, but in themselves.*

I tell the man who doubts the power of the Bible, because many read it, and are no better for the reading, that the abuse of a thing is no argument against the use of it. I tell him boldly, that never did man or woman read that book in a childlike persevering spirit—like the Ethiopian eunuch, and the Bereans (Acts 8:28; 18:11)—and miss the way to heaven. Yes, many a broken cistern will be exposed to shame in the day of judgment; but there will not rise up one soul who will be able to say, that he went thirsting to the Bible, and found in it no living water—he searched for truth in the Scriptures, and searching, did not find it. The words which are spoken of wisdom in the Proverbs are strictly true of the Bible: "If thou criest after knowledge, and liftest up thy voice for understanding; if thou seekest her as silver, and searchest for her as for hid treasures; then shalt thou understand the fear of the Lord, and find the knowledge of God" (Prov. 2:3-5).

This wonderful book is the subject about which I address the readers of this paper this day. Surely it is no light matter *what you are doing with the Bible*. What should you think of the man who in time of cholera despised a sure receipt for preserving the health of his body? What must be thought of you if you despise the only sure receipt for the everlasting health of your soul? I charge you, I entreat you, to give an honest answer to my question. What dost thou do with the Bible? Dost thou read it? HOW READEST THOU?

VI. In the sixth place, *the Bible is the only rule by which all questions of doctrine or of duty can be tried*.

The Lord God knows the weakness and infirmity of our poor fallen understandings. He knows that, even after conversion, our perceptions of right and wrong are exceedingly indistinct. He knows how artfully Satan can gild error with an appearance of truth, and can dress up wrong with plausible arguments, till it looks like right. Knowing all this, He has mercifully provided us with an unerring standard of truth and error, right and wrong, and has taken care to make that standard a written book—even the Scripture.

No one can look round the world, and not see the wisdom of such a provision. No one can live long, and not find out that he is constantly in need of a counselor and adviser, of a rule of faith and practice, on which he can depend. Unless he lives like a beast, without a soul and conscience, he will find himself constantly assailed by difficult and puzzling questions. He will be often asking himself, What must I believe? And what must I do?

(a) The world is full of difficulties about points of *doctrine*. The house of error lies close alongside the house of truth. The door of one is so like the door of the other that there is continual risk of mistakes.

Does a man read or travel much? He will soon find the most opposite opinions prevailing among those who are called Christians. He will discover that different persons give the most different answers to the important question, What shall I do to be saved? The Roman Catholic and the Protestant, the Neologian and the Tractarian, the Mormonite and the Swedenborgian—each and all will assert that he alone has the truth. Each and all will tell him that safety is only to be found in his party. Each and all say, "Come with us." All this is puzzling. What shall a man do?

Does he settle down quietly in some English or Scotch parish? He will soon find that even in our own land the most conflicting views are held. He will soon discover that there are serious differences among Christians as to the comparative importance of the various parts and articles of the faith. One man thinks of nothing but church government, another of nothing but sacraments, services, and forms, a third of nothing but preaching the gospel. Does he apply to ministers for a solution? He will perhaps find one minister teaching one doctrine, and another another. All this is puzzling. What shall a man do?

There is only one answer to this question. A man must make the Bible alone his rule. He must receive nothing, and believe nothing, which is not according to the Word. He must try all religious teaching by one simple test—Does it square with the Bible? What saith the Scripture?

I would to God the eyes of the laity of this country were more open on this subject. I would to God they would learn to weigh sermons, books, opinions, and ministers, on the scales of the Bible, and to value all according to their conformity to the Word. I would to God they would see that it matters little who says a thing—whether he be Father or Reformer, Bishop or Archbishop, Priest or Deacon, Archdeacon or Dean. The only question is, Is the thing said scriptural? If it is, it ought to be received and believed. If it is not, it ought to be refused and cast aside. I fear the consequences of that servile acceptance of everything which ''the parson'' says, which is so common among many English laymen. I fear lest they be led they know not whither, like the blinded Syrians, and awake some day to find themselves in the power of Rome (II Kings 6:20). Oh, that men in England would only remember for what purpose the Bible was given them!

I tell English laymen that it is nonsense to say, as some do, that it is presumptuous to judge a minister's teaching by the Word. When one doctrine is proclaimed in one parish, and another in another, people must read and judge for themselves. Both doctrines cannot be right, and both ought to be tried by the Word. I charge them, above all things, never to suppose that any true minister of the gospel will dislike his people measuring all he teaches by the Bible. On the contrary, the more they read the Bible, and prove all he says by the Bible, the better he will be pleased. A false minister may say, ''You have no right to use your private judgment; leave the Bible to us who are ordained.'' A true minister will say, "Search the Scriptures, and if I do not teach you what is scriptural, do not believe me." A false minister may cry, "Hear the church," and "Hear me." A true minister will say, "Hear the Word of God."

(b) But the world is not only full of difficulties about points of doctrine; it is equally full of difficulties about points of *practice*. Every professing Christian, who wishes to act conscientiously, must know that it is so. The most puzzling questions are continually arising. He is tried on every side by doubts as to the line of duty, and can often hardly see what is the right thing to do.

He is tried by questions connected with the management of his *worldly calling*, if he is in business or in trade. He sometimes sees things going on of a very doubtful character—things that can hardly be called fair, straightforward, truthful, and doing as you would be done by. But then everybody in the trade does these things. They have always been done in the most respectable houses. There would be no carrying on a profitable business if they were not done. They are not things distinctly named and prohibited by God. All this is very puzzling. What is a man to do?

He is tried by questions about *worldly amusements*. Races, and balls, and operas, and theaters, and card parties, are all very doubtful methods of spending time. But then he sees numbers of great people taking part in them. Are all these people wrong? Can there really be such mighty harm in these things? All this is very puzzling. What is a man to do?

He is tried by questions about the *education of his children*. He wishes to train them up morally and religiously, and to remember their souls. But he is told by many sensible people, that young persons will be young, that it does not do to check and restrain them too much, and that he ought to attend pantomimes and children's parties, and give children's balls himself. He is informed that this nobleman, or that lady of rank, always does so, and yet they are reckoned religious people. Surely it cannot be wrong. All this is very puzzling. What is he to do?

There is only one answer to all these questions. A man must make the Bible his rule of conduct. He must make its leading principles the compass by which he steers his course through life. By the letter or spirit of the Bible he must test every difficult point and question. *"To the law and to the testimony! What saith the Scripture?"* He ought to care nothing for what other people may think right. He ought not to set his watch by the clock of his neighbor, but by the sundial of the Word.

I charge my readers solemnly to act on the maxim I have just laid down, and to adhere to it rigidly all the days of their lives. You will never repent of it. Make it a leading principle never to act contrary to the Word. Care not for the charge of over-strictness, and needless precision. Remember you serve a strict and holy God. Listen not to the common objection, that the rule you have laid down is impossible, and cannot be observed in such a world as this. Let those who make such an objection speak out plainly, and tell us for what purpose the Bible was given to man. Let them remember that by the Bible we shall all be judged at the last day, and let them learn to judge themselves by it here, lest they be judged and condemned by it hereafter.

This mighty rule of faith and practice is the book about which I am addressing the readers of this paper this day. Surely it is no light matter *what you are doing with the Bible.* Surely when danger is abroad on the right hand and on the left, you should consider what you are doing with the safeguard which God has provided. I charge you, I beseech you, to give an honest answer to my question. What art thou doing with the Bible? Dost thou read it? HOW READEST THOU?

VII. In the seventh place, *the Bible is the book which all true servants of God have always lived on and loved.*

Every living thing which God creates requires food. The life that God imparts needs sustaining and nourishing. It is so with animal and vegetable life, with birds, beasts, fishes, reptiles, insects, and plants. It is equally so with spiritual life. When the Holy Ghost raises a man from the death of sin and makes him a new creature in Christ Jesus, the new principle in that man's heart requires food, and the only food which will sustain it is the Word of God.

There never was a man or woman truly converted, from one end of the world to the other, who did not love the revealed will of God. Just as a child born into the world desires naturally the milk provided for its nourishment, so does a soul "born again" desire the sincere milk of the Word. This is a common mark of all the children of God—they "delight in the law of the Lord" (Ps. 1:2).

Show me a person who despises Bible reading, or thinks little of Bible preaching, and I hold it to be a certain fact that he is not yet "born again." He may be zealous about forms and ceremonies. He may be diligent in attending sacraments and daily services. But if these things are more precious to him than the Bible, I cannot think he is a converted man. Tell me what the Bible is to a man, and I will generally tell you what he is. This is the pulse to try, this is the barometer to look at, if we would know the state of the heart. I have no notion of the Spirit dwelling in a man and not giving clear evidence of His presence. And I believe it to be a signal evidence of the Spirit's presence when the Word is really precious to a man's soul.

Love of the Word is one of the characteristics we see in Job. Little as we know of this patriarch and his age, this at least stands out clearly. He says, "I have esteemed the words of his mouth more than my necessary food" (Job 23:12).

Love of the Word is a shining feature in the character of David. Mark how it appears all through that wonderful part of Scripture, the 119th Psalm. He might well say, "Oh, how I love thy law!" (Ps. 119:97).

Love of the Word is a striking point in the character of St. Paul. What were he and his companions but men "mighty in the Scriptures?" What were his sermons but expositions and applications of the Word?

Love of the Word appears preeminently in our Lord and Savior Jesus Christ. He read it publicly. He quoted it continually. He expounded it frequently. He advised the Jews to "search" it. He used it as His weapon to resist the devil. He said repeatedly, "The Scripture must be fulfilled." Almost the last thing He did was to "open the understanding of his disciples, that they might understand the scriptures" (Luke 24:45). I am afraid that man can be no true servant of Christ, who has not something of his Master's mind and feeling towards the Bible.

Love of the Word has been a prominent feature in the history of all the saints, of whom we know anything, since the days of the apostles. This is the lamp which Athanasius and Chrysostom and Augustine followed. This is the compass which kept the Vallenses and Albigenses from making shipwreck of the faith. This is the well which was reopened by Wycliffe and Luther, after it had been long stopped up. This is the sword with which Latimer, and Jewell, and Knox won their victories. This is the manna which fed Baxter and Owen, and the noble host of the Puritans, and made them strong to battle. This is the armory from which Whitefield and Wesley drew their powerful weapons. This is the mine from which Bickersteth and McCheyne brought forth rich gold. Differing as these holy men did in some matters, on one point they were all agreed—they all delighted in the Word.

Love of the Word is one of the first things that appears in the converted heathen, at the various missionary stations throughout the world. In hot climates and in cold, among savage people and among civilized, in New Zealand, in the South Sea Islands, in Africa, in Hindostan—it is always the same. They enjoy hearing it read. They long to be able to read it themselves. They wonder why Christians did not send it to them before. How striking is the picture which Moffat draws of Afrikaner, the fierce South African chieftain, when first brought under the power of the gospel! "Often have I seen him," he says, "under the shadow of a great rock nearly the live-long day, eagerly perusing the pages of the Bible." How touching is the expression of a poor converted Negro, speaking of the Bible! He said, "It is never old and never cold." How affecting was the language of another old Negro, when some would have dissuaded him from learning to read, because of his great age. "No!" he said, "I will never give it up till I die. It is worth all the labor to be able to read that one verse, 'God so loved the world, that he gave his only begotten Son, that whosoever believeth in him should not perish, but have eternal life.' "

Love of the Bible is one of the grand points of agreement among all converted men and women in our own land. Episcopalians and Presbyterians, Baptists and Independents, Methodists and Plymouth Brethren—all unite in honoring the Bible, as soon as they are real Christians. This is the manna which all the tribes of our Israel feed upon, and find satisfying food. This is the fountain round which all the various portions of Christ's flock meet together, and from which no sheep goes thirsty away. Oh, that believers in this country would learn to cleave more closely to the written Word! Oh, that they would see that the more the Bible, and the Bible only, is the substance of men's religion, the more they agree! It is probable there never was an uninspired book more universally admired than Bunyan's *Pilgrim's Progress*. It is a book which all denominations of Christians delight to honor. It has won praise from all parties. Now what a striking fact it is, that the author was preeminently a man of one book! He had read hardly anything but the Bible.

It is a blessed thought that there will be "much people" in heaven at last. Few as the Lord's people undoubtedly are at any one given time or place, yet all gathered together at last, they will be "a multitude that no man can number" (Rev. 7:9; 19:1). They will be of one heart and mind. They will have passed through like experience. They will all have repented, believed, lived holy, prayerful, and humble. They will all have washed their robes and made them white in the blood of the Lamb. But one thing beside all this they will have in common: they will all love the texts and doctrines of the Bible. The Bible will have been their food and delight in the days of their pilgrimage on earth. And the Bible will be a common subject of joyful meditation and retrospect, when they are gathered together in heaven.

This book, which all true Christians live upon and love, is the subject about which I am addressing the readers of this paper this day. Surely it is no light matter *what you are doing with the Bible.* Surely it is a matter for serious inquiry, whether you know anything of this love to the Word, and have this mark of walking "in the footsteps of the flock" (Cant. 1:8). I charge you, I entreat you to give me an honest answer. What art thou doing with the Bible? Dost thou read it? HOW READEST THOU?

VIII. In the last place, *the Bible is the only book which can comfort a man in the last hours of his life.*

Death is an event which in all probability is before us all. There is no avoiding it. It is the river which each of us must cross. I who write, and you who read, have each one day to die. It is good to remember this. We are all sadly apt to put away the subject from us. "Each man thinks each man mortal but himself." I want every one to do his duty in life, but I also want every one to think of death. I want every one to know how to live, but I also want every one to know how to die.

Death is a solemn event to all. It is the winding up of all earthly plans and expectations. It is a separation from all we have loved and lived with. It is often accompanied by much bodily pain and distress. It brings us to the grave, the worm, and corruption. It opens the door to judgment and eternity, to heaven or to hell. It is an event after which there is no change, or space for repentance. Other mistakes may be corrected or retrieved, but not a mistake on our deathbeds. As the tree falls, there it must lie. No conversion in the coffin! No new birth after we have ceased to breathe! And death is before us all. It may be close at hand. The time of our departure is quite uncertain. But sooner or later we must each lie down alone and die. All these are serious considerations.

Death is a solemn event even to the believer in Christ. For him no doubt the "sting of death" is taken away (I Cor. 15:55). Death has become one of his privileges, for he is Christ's. Living or dying, he is the Lord's. If he lives, Christ lives in him; and if he dies, he goes to live with Christ. To him "to live is Christ, and to die is gain" (Phil. 1:21). Death frees him from many trials—from a weak body, a corrupt heart, a tempting devil, and an ensnaring or persecuting world. Death admits him to the enjoyment of many blessings. He rests from his labors; the hope of a joyful resurrection is changed into a certainty; he has the company of holy redeemed spirits; he is "with Christ." All this is true, and yet, even to a believer, death is a solemn thing. Flesh and blood naturally shrink from it. To part from all we love, is a wrench and trial to the feelings. The world we go to is a world unknown, even though it is our home. Friendly and harmless as death is to a believer, it is not an event to be treated lightly. It always must be a very solemn thing.

It becomes every thoughtful and sensible man to consider calmly how he is going to meet death. Gird up your loins, like a man, and look the subject in the face. Listen to me, while I tell you a few things about the end to which we are coming.

The good things of the world cannot comfort a man when he draws near death. All the gold of California and Australia will not provide light for the dark valley. Money can buy the best medical advice and attendance for a man's body; but money cannot buy peace for his conscience, heart, and soul.

Relatives, loved friends, and servants, cannot comfort a man when he draws near death. They may minister affectionately to his bodily wants. They may watch by his bedside tenderly, and anticipate his every wish. They may smooth down his dying pillow, and support his sinking frame in their arms. But they cannot "minister to a mind diseased.'' They cannot stop the achings of a troubled heart. They cannot screen an uneasy conscience from the eye of God.

The pleasures of the world cannot comfort a man when he draws near death. The brilliant ballroom, the merry dance, the midnight revel, the party to Epsom races, the card table, the box at the opera, the voices of singing men and singing women—all these are at length distasteful things. To hear of hunting and shooting engagements gives him no pleasure. To be invited to feasts, and regattas, and facy fairs, gives him no ease. He cannot hide from himself that these are hollow, empty, powerless things. They jar upon the ear of his conscience. They are out of harmony with his condition. They cannot stop one gap in his heart, when the last enemy is coming in like a flood. They cannot make him calm in the prospect of meeting a holy God.

Books and newspapers cannot comfort a man when he draws near death. The most brilliant writings of Macaulay or Dickens will pall on his ear. The most able article in the *Times* will fail to interest him. The *Edinburgh* and *Quarterly Review* will give him no pleasure. *Punch* and the *Illustrated News,* and the last new novel, will lie unopened and unheeded. Their time will be past. Their vocation will be gone. Whatever they may be in health, they are useless in the hour of death.

There is but one fountain of comfort for a man drawing near to his end, and that is the Bible. Chapters out of the Bible, texts out of the Bible, statements of truth taken out of the Bible, books containing matter drawn from the Bible, these are a man's only chance of comfort when he comes to die. I do not at all say that the Bible will do good, as a matter of course, to a dying man, if he has not valued it before. I know, unhappily, too much of deathbeds to say that. I do not say whether it is probable that he who has been unbelieving and neglectful of the Bible in life, will at once believe and get comfort from it in death. But I do say positively, that no dying man will ever get real comfort, except from the contents of the Word of God. All comfort from any other source is a house built upon sand.

I lay this down as a rule of universal application. I make no exception in favor of any class on earth. Kings and poor men, learned and unlearned—all are on a level in this matter. There is not a jot of real consolation for any dying man, unless he gets it from the Bible. Chapters, passages, texts, promises, and doctrines of Scripture—heard, received, believed, and rested on—these are the only comforters I dare promise to any one, when he leaves the world. Taking the sacrament will do a man no more good than the popish extreme unction, so long as the Word is not received and believed. Priestly absolution will no more ease the conscience than the incantations of a heathen magician, if the poor dying sinner does not receive and believe Bible truth. I tell every one who reads this paper, that although men may seem to get on comfortably without the Bible while they live, they may be sure that without the Bible they cannot comfortably die. It was a true confession of the learned Selden, "There is no book upon which we can rest in a dying moment but the Bible."

I might easily confirm all I have just said, by examples and illustrations. I might show you the deathbeds of men who have affected to despise the Bible. I might tell you how Voltaire and Paine, the famous infidels, died in misery, bitterness, rage, fear, and despair. I might show you the happy deathbeds of those who have loved the Bible and believed it, and the blessed effect the sight of their deathbeds had on others. Cecil, a minister whose praise ought to be in all churches, says, "I shall never forget standing by the bedside of my dying mother. 'Are you afraid to die?' I asked. 'No!' she replied. 'But why does the uncertainty of another state give you no concern?' 'Because God has said, "Fear not; when thou passest through the waters, I will be with thee; and through the rivers, they shall not overflow thee" ' " (Isa. 43:1, 2). I might easily multiply illustrations of this kind. But I think it better to conclude this part of my subject by giving the result of my own observations as a minister.

I have seen not a few dying persons in my time. I have seen great varieties of manner and deportment among them. I have seen some die sullen, silent, and comfortless. I have seen others die ignorant, unconcerned, and apparently without much fear. I have seen some die so wearied out with long illness that they were quite willing to depart, and yet they did not seem to me at all in a fit state to go before God. I have seen others die with professions of hope and trust in God, without leaving satisfactory evidences that they were on the rock. I have seen others die who, I believe, were "in Christ," and safe, and yet they never seemed to enjoy much sensible comfort. I have seen some few dying in the full assurance of hope, and like Bunyan's Standfast, giving glorious testimony to Christ's faithfulness, even in the river. But one thing I have never seen. I never saw any one enjoy what I should call real, solid, calm, reasonable peace on his deathbed, who did not draw his peace from the Bible. And this I am bold to say, that the man who thinks to go to his deathbed without having the Bible for his comforter, his companion, and his friend, is one of the greatest madmen in the world. There are no comforts for the soul but Bible comforts, and he who has not got hold of these, has got hold of nothing at all, unless it be a broken reed.

The only comforter for a deathbed is the book about which I address the readers of this paper this day. Surely it is no light matter whether you read that book or not. Surely a dying man, in a dying world, should seriously consider whether he has got anything to comfort him when his turn comes to die. I charge you, I entreat you, for the last time, to give an honest answer to my question. What art thou doing with the Bible? Dost thou read it? HOW READEST THOU?

I have now given the reasons why I press on every reader the duty and importance of reading the Bible. I have shown that no book is written in such a manner as the Bible, that knowledge of the Bible is absolutely necessary to salvation, that no book contains such matter, that no book has done so much for the world generally, that no book can do so much for every one who reads it aright, that this book is the only rule of faith and practice, that it is, and always has been, the food of all true servants of God, and that it is the only book which can comfort men when they die. All these are ancient things. I do not pretend to tell anything new. I have only gathered together old truths, and tried to mold them into a new shape. Let me finish all by addressing a few plain words to the conscience of every class of readers.

(1) This paper may fall into the hands of some who *can read, but never do read the Bible at all.* Are you one of them? If you are, I have something to say to you.

I cannot comfort you in your present state of mind. It would be mockery and deceit to do so. I cannot speak to you of peace and heaven, while you treat the Bible as you do. You are in danger of losing your soul.

You are in danger, because *your neglected Bible is a plain evidence that you do not love God.* The health of a man's body may generally be known by his appetite.

The health of a man's soul may be known by his treatment of the Bible. Now you are manifestly laboring under a sore disease. Will you not repent?

I know I cannot reach your heart. I cannot make you see and feel these things. I can only enter my solemn protest against your present treatment of the Bible, and lay that protest before your conscience. I do so with all my soul. Oh, beware lest you repent too late! Beware lest you put off reading the Bible till you send for the doctor in your last illness, and then find the Bible a sealed book, and dark, as the cloud between the hosts of Israel and Egypt, to your anxious soul! Beware lest you go on saying, all your life, "Men do very well without all this Bible reading," and find at length, to your cost, that men do very ill, and end in hell! Beware lest the day come when you will feel, "Had I but honored the Bible as much as I have honored the newspaper, I should not have been left without comfort in my last hours!" Bible-neglecting reader, I give you a plain warning. The plague-cross is at present on your door. The Lord have mercy upon your soul!

(2) This paper may fall into the hands of some one who is *willing to begin reading the Bible, but wants advice* on the subject. Are you that man? Listen to me, and I will give a few short hints.

(a) For one thing, *begin reading your Bible this very day*. The way to do a thing is to do it, and the way to read the Bible is actually to read it. It is not meaning, or wishing, or resolving, or intending, or thinking about it, which will advance you one step. You must positively read. There is no royal road in this matter, any more than in the matter of prayer. If you cannot read yourself, you must persuade somebody else to read to you. But one way or another, through eyes or ears, the words of Scripture must actually pass before your mind.

(b) For another thing, *read the Bible with an earnest desire to understand it*. Think not for a moment that the great object is to turn over a certain quantity of printed paper, and that it matters nothing whether you understand it or not. Some ignorant people seem to fancy that all is done if they clear off so many chapters every day, though they may not have a notion what they are all about, and only know that they have pushed on their mark so many leaves. This is turning Bible reading into a mere form. It is almost as bad as the popish habit of buying indulgences, by saying an almost fabulous number of ave marias and paternosters. It reminds one of the poor Hottentot who ate up a Dutch hymnbook because he saw it comforted his neighbors' hearts. Settle it down in your mind as a general principle, that a Bible not understood is a Bible that does no good. Say to yourself often as you read, "What is all this about?" Dig for the meaning like a man digging for Australian gold. Work hard, and do not give up the work in a hurry.

(c) For another thing, *read the Bible with childlike faith and humility*. Open your heart as you open your book, and say, "Speak, Lord, for thy servant heareth." Resolve to believe implicitly whatever you find there, however much it may run counter to your own prejudices. Resolve to receive heartily every statement of truth, whether you like it or not. Beware of that miserable habit of mind into which some readers of the Bible fall. They receive some doctrines because they like them; they reject others because they are condemning to themselves, or to some lover, or relation, or friend. At this rate the Bible is useless. Are we to be judges of what ought to be in the Word? Do we know better than God? Settle it down in your mind that you will receive all and believe all, and that what you cannot understand you will take on trust. Remember, when you pray, you are

speaking to God, and God hears you. But, remember, when you read, God is speaking to you, and you are not to "answer again," but to listen.

(d) For another thing, *read the Bible in a spirit of obedience and self-application*. Sit down to the study of it with a daily determination that *you* will live by its rules, rest on its statements, and act on its commands. Consider, as you travel through every chapter, "How does this affect *my* position and course of conduct? What does this teach *me?*" It is poor work to read the Bible from mere curiosity, and for speculative purposes, in order to fill your head and store your mind with opinions, while you do not allow the book to influence your heart and life. That Bible is read best which is practiced most.

(e) For another thing, *read the Bible daily*. Make it a part of every day's business to read and meditate on some portion of God's Word. Private means of grace are just as needful every day for our souls as food and clothing are for our bodies. Yesterday's bread will not feed the laborer today, and today's bread will not feed the laborer tomorrow. Do as the Israelites did in the wilderness. Gather your manna fresh every morning. Choose your own seasons and hours. Do not scramble over and hurry your reading. Give your Bible the best and not the worst part of your time. But whatever plan you pursue, let it be a rule of your life to visit the throne of grace and the Bible every day.

(f) For another thing, *read all the Bible, and read it in an orderly way*. I fear there are many parts of the Word which some people never read at all. This is to say the least, a very presumptuous habit. "All scripture is profitable" (II Tim. 3:16). To this habit may be traced that want of broad, well-proportioned views of truth, which is so common in this day. Some people's Bible

reading is a system of perpetual dipping and picking. They do not seem to have an idea of regularly going through the whole book. This also is a great mistake. No doubt in times of sickness and affliction it is allowable to search out seasonable portions. But with this exception, I believe it is by far the best plan to begin the Old and New Testaments at the same time—to read each straight through to the end, and then begin again. This is a matter in which every one must be persuaded in his own mind. I can only say it has been my own plan for nearly forty years, and I have never seen cause to alter it.

(g) For another thing, *read the Bible fairly and honestly.* Determine to take everything in its plain, obvious meaning, and regard all forced interpretations with great suspicion. As a general rule, whatever a verse of the Bible seems to mean, it does mean. Cecil's rule is a very valuable one, ''The right way of interpreting Scripture is to take it as we find it, without any attempt to force it into any particular system.'' Well said Hooker, ''I hold it for a most infallible rule in the exposition of Scripture, that when a literal construction will stand, the furthest from the literal is commonly the worst.''

(h) In the last place, *read the Bible with Christ continually in view.* The grand primary object of all Scripture is to testify of Jesus. Old Testament ceremonies are shadows of Christ. Old Testament judges and deliverers are types of Christ. Old Testament history shows the world's need of Christ. Old Testament prophecies are full of Christ's sufferings, and of Christ's glory yet to come. The first advent and the second, the Lord's humiliation and the Lord's kingdom, the cross and the crown, shine forth everywhere in the Bible. Keep fast hold on this clue, if you would read the Bible aright.

I might easily add to these hints, if space permitted. Few and short as they are, you will find them worth attention. Act upon them, and I firmly believe you will never be allowed to miss the way to heaven. Act upon them, and you will find light continually increasing in your mind. No book of evidence can be compared with that internal evidence which he obtains who daily uses the Word in the right way. Such a man does not need the books of learned men, like Paley, and Wilson, and M'Ilvaine. He has the witness in himself. The book satisfies and feeds his soul. A poor Christian woman once said to an infidel, ''I am no scholar. I cannot argue like you. But I know that honey is honey, because it leaves a sweet taste in my mouth. And I know the Bible to be God's book, because of the taste it leaves in my heart.''

(3) This paper may fall into the hands of some one who *loves and believes the Bible, and yet reads it but little*. I fear there are many such in this day. It is a day of bustle and hurry. It is a day of talking, and committee meetings, and public work. These things are all very well in their way, but I fear that they sometimes clip and cut short the private reading of the Bible. Does your conscience tell you that you are one of the persons I speak of? Listen to me, and I will say a few things which deserve your serious attention.

You are the man that is likely to *get little comfort from the Bible in time of need*. Trial is a sifting season. Affliction is a searching wind, which strips the leaves off the trees, and brings to light the birds' nests. Now I fear that your stores of Bible consolations may one day run very low. I fear lest you should find yourself at last on very short allowance, and come into harbor weak, worn, and thin.

You are the man that is likely *never to be established in the truth*. I shall not be surprised to hear that you are troubled with doubts and questionings about assurance, grace, faith, perseverance, and the like. The devil is an old and cunning enemy. Like the Benjamites, he can "throw stones at a hair breadth, and not miss" (Judg. 20:16). He can quote Scripture readily enough when he pleases. Now you are not sufficiently ready with your weapons to be able to fight a good fight with him. Your armor does not fit you well. Your sword sits loosely in your hand.

You are the man that is likely to *make mistakes in life*. I shall not wonder if I am told that you have erred about your own marriage, erred about your children's education, erred about the conduct of your household, erred about the company you keep. The world you steer through is full of rocks, and shoals, and sandbanks. You are not sufficiently familiar either with the lights or charts.

You are the man that is likely to *be carried away by some specious false teacher for a season*. It will not surprise me if I hear that some one of those clever, eloquent men, who can "make the worse appear the better cause," is leading you into many follies. You are wanting in ballast. No wonder if you are tossed to and fro, like a cork on the waves.

All these are uncomfortable things. I want every reader of this paper to escape them all. Take the advice I offer you this day. Do not merely read your Bible "a little," but read it a great deal. "Let the word of Christ dwell in you richly" (Col. 3:16). Do not be a mere babe in spiritual knowledge. Seek to become "well instructed in the kingdom of heaven," and to be continually adding new things to old. A religion of feeling is an uncertain thing. It is like the tide, sometimes high, and sometimes low. It is like the moon, sometimes bright, and sometimes dim. A religion of deep Bible knowledge, is a firm and lasting possession. It enables a man not merely to say, "I feel hope in Christ," but "I know whom I have believed" (II Tim. 1:12).

(4) This paper may fall into the hands of some one who *reads the Bible much, and yet fancies he is no better for his reading*. This is a crafty temptation of the devil. At one stage he says, "Do not read the Bible at all." At another he says, "Your reading does you no good; give it up." Are you that man? I feel for you from the bottom of my soul. Let me try to do you good.

Do not think you are getting no good from the Bible, merely because you do not see that good day by day. The greatest effects are by no means those which make the most noise, and are most easily observed. The greatest effects are often silent, quiet, and hard to detect at the time they are being produced. Think of the influence of the moon upon the earth, and of the air upon the human lungs. Remember how silently the dew falls, and how imperceptibly the grass grows. There may be far more doing than you think in your soul by your Bible reading.

The Word may be gradually producing deep *impressions* on your heart, of which you are not at present aware. Often when the memory is retaining no facts, the character of a man is receiving some everlasting impression. Is sin becoming every year more hateful to you? Is Christ becoming every year more precious? Is holiness becoming every year more lovely and desirable in your eyes? If these things are so, take courage. The Bible is doing you good, though you may not be able to trace it out day by day.

The Bible may be restraining you from some sin or delusion into which you would otherwise run. It may be daily keeping you back, and hedging you up, and preventing many a false step. Ah, you might soon find this out to your cost, if you were to cease reading the Word! The very familiarity of blessings sometimes makes us insensible to their value. Resist the devil. Settle it down in your mind as an established rule, that, whether you feel it at the moment or not, you are inhaling spiritual health by reading the Bible, and insensibly becoming more strong.

(5) This paper may fall into the hands of some who *really love the Bible, live upon the Bible, and read it much*. Are you one of these? Give me your attention, and I will mention a few things which we shall do well to lay to heart for time to come.

Let us resolve to *read the Bible more and more* every year we live. Let us try to get it rooted in our memories, and engrafted into our hearts. Let us be thoroughly well provisioned with it against the voyage of death. Who knows but we may have a very stormy passage? Sight and hearing may fail us, and we may be in deep waters. Oh, to have the Word "hid in our hearts" in such an hour as that! (Ps. 119:11).

Let us resolve to be *more watchful over our Bible reading* every year that we live. Let us be jealously careful about the time we give to it, and the manner that time is spent. Let us beware of omitting our daily reading without sufficient cause. Let us not be gaping, and yawning, and dozing over our book, while we read. Let us read like a London merchant studying the city article in the Times, or like a wife reading a husband's letter from a distant land. Let us be very careful that we never exalt any minister, or sermon, or book, or tract, or friend above the Word. Cursed be that book, or tract, or human counsel, which creeps in between us and the Bible, and hides the Bible from our eyes! Once more I say, let us be very watchful. The moment we open the Bible the devil sits down by our side. Oh, to read with a hungry spirit, and a simple desire for edification!

Let us resolve to *honor the Bible more in our families*. Let us read it morning and evening to our children and households, and not be ashamed to let men see that we do so. Let us not be discouraged by seeing no good arise from it. The Bible reading in a family has kept many a one from the jail, the workhouse, and the *Gazette*, if it has not kept him from hell.

Let us resolve to *meditate more on the Bible*. It is good to take with us two or three texts when we go out into the world, and to turn them over and over in our minds whenever we have a little leisure. It keeps out many vain thoughts. It clenches the nail of daily reading. It preserves our souls from stagnating and breeding corrupt things. It sanctifies and quickens our memories, and prevents them becoming like those ponds where the frogs live but the fish die.

Let us resolve to *talk more to believers about the Bible* when we meet them. Alas, the conversation of Christians, when they do meet, is often sadly unprofitable! How many frivolous, and trifling, and uncharitable things are said! Let us bring out the Bible more, and it will help to drive the devil away, and keep our hearts in tune. Oh, that we may all strive so to walk together in this evil world, that Jesus may often draw near, and go with us, as He went with the two disciples journeying to Emmaus!

Last of all, let us resolve to *live by the Bible more and more* every year we live. Let us frequently take account of all our opinions and practices, of our habits and tempers, of our behavior in public and in private, in the world, and by our own firesides. Let us measure all by the Bible, and resolve, by God's help, to conform to it. Oh, that we may learn increasingly to "cleanse our ways" by the Word! (Ps. 119:9).

I commend all these things to the serious and prayerful attention of every one into whose hands this paper may fall. I want the ministers of my beloved country to be Bible-reading ministers, the congregations, Bible-reading congregations, and the nation, a Bible-reading nation. To bring about this desirable end I cast in my mite into God's treasury. The Lord grant that it may prove not to have been in vain!

7

The Church Which Christ Builds

"Upon this rock I will build my church; and the gates of hell shall not prevail against it."—
Matt. 16:18

Do we belong to the church which is built upon a rock? Are we members of the only church in which our souls can be saved? These are serious questions. They deserve serious consideration. I ask the attention of all who read this paper, while I try to show the one true, holy, catholic church, and to guide men's feet into the only safe fold. "What is this church? What is it like? What are its marks? Where is it to be found?" On all these points I have somewhat to say. I am going to unfold the words of our Lord Jesus Christ, which stand at the head of this page. He declares, "Upon this rock I will build my church; and the gates of hell shall not prevail against it."

There are five things in these famous words which demand our attention:

I. *A Building:* "My church."
II. *A Builder:* Christ says, "I will build my church."

179

III. *A Foundation:* "Upon this rock I will build my church."

IV. *Perils Implied:* "The gates of hell."

V. *Security Asserted:* "The gates of hell shall not prevail against it."

The whole subject demands special attention in the present day. Holiness, we must never forget, is the prominent characteristic of all who belong to the one true church.

I. We have, firstly, a *Building* mentioned in the text. The Lord Jesus Christ speaks of "my church."

Now what is this church? Few inquiries can be made of more importance than this. For want of due attention to this subject, the errors that have crept into the world are neither few nor small.

The church of our text is no material building. It is no temple made with hands of wood, or brick, or stone, or marble. It is a company of men and women. It is no particular visible church on earth. It is not the Eastern Church or the Western Church. It is not the Church of England or the Church of Scotland. Above all, it certainly is not the Church of Rome. The church of our text is one that makes far less show than any visible church in the eyes of man, but is of far more importance in the eyes of God.

The church of our text is made up of all true believers in the Lord Jesus Christ, of all who are really holy, and converted people. It comprehends all who have repented of sin, and fled to Christ by faith, and been made new creatures in Him. It comprises all God's elect, all who have received God's grace, all who have been washed in Christ's blood, all who have been clothed in

Christ's righteousness, all who have been born again and sanctified by Christ's Spirit. All such, of every name, and rank, and nation, and people, and tongue, compose the church of our text. This is the body of Christ. This is the flock of Christ. This is the bride. This is the Lamb's wife. This is "the holy Catholic and Apostolic Church" of the Apostle's Creed, and the Nicene Creed. This is "the blessed company of all faithful people," spoken of in the communion service of the Church of England. This is "THE CHURCH ON THE ROCK."

The members of this church do not all worship God in the same way, or use the same form of government. Some of them are governed by bishops, and some of them by elders. Some of them use a prayerbook when they meet for public worship, and some of them use none. The thirty-fourth article of the Church of England most wisely declares, "It is not necessary that ceremonies should be in all places one and alike." But the members of this church all come to one throne of grace. They all worship with one heart. They are all led by one Spirit. They are all really and truly *holy*. They can all say "Alleluia," and they can all reply, "Amen."

This is that church, to which all visible churches on earth are servants and handmaidens. Whether they are Episcopalian, Independent, or Presbyterian, they all serve the intersts of the one true church. They are the scaffolding, behind which the great building is carried on. They are the husk, under which the living kernel grows. They have their various degrees of usefulness. The best and worthiest of them is that which trains up most members for Christ's true church. But no visible church has any right to say, "We are the only True Church. We are the men, and wisdom shall die with us." No visible church should ever dare to say, "We shall stand forever. The gates of hell shall not prevail against me."

This is that church to which belong the Lord's gracious promises of preservation, continuance, protection, and final glory. "Whatsoever," says Hooker, "we read in Scripture, concerning the endless love and saving mercy, which God showeth towards His Churches, the only proper subject thereof is this Church, which we properly term the mystical body of Christ." Small and despised as the true church may be in this world, it is precious and honorable in the sight of God. The temple of Solomon in all its glory was mean and contemptible, in comparison with that church which is built upon a rock.

I trust the things I have just been saying will sink down into the minds of all who read this paper. See that you hold sound doctrine upon the subject of "the church." A mistake here may lead on to dangerous and soul-ruining errors. The church which is made up of true believers, is the church for which we, who are ministers, are specially ordained to preach. The church which comprises all who repent and believe the gospel, is the church to which we desire you to belong. Our work is not done, and our hearts are not satisfied, until you are made a new creature, and are a member of the one true church. Outside of the church which is "built on the rock" there can be NO SALVATION.

II. I pass on to the second point, to which I proposed to invite your attention. Our text contains not merely a building, but a *Builder*. The Lord Jesus Christ declares, "*I* will build my church."

The true church of Christ is tenderly cared for by all the three persons of the blessed Trinity. In the plan of salvation revealed in the Bible, beyond doubt, God the Father chooses, God the Son redeems, and God the Holy Ghost sanctifies every member of Christ's mystical body. God the Father, God the Son, and God the Holy Ghost, three persons and one God, cooperate for the salvation of every saved soul. This is truth, which ought never to be forgotten. Nevertheless, there is a peculiar sense in which the help of the church is laid on the Lord Jesus Christ. He is peculiarly and preeminently the Redeemer and Savior of the church. Therefore it is, that we find Him saying in our text, ''I will build—the work of building is my special work.''

It is Christ who calls the members of the church in due time. They are ''the called of Jesus Christ'' (Rom. 1:6). It is Christ who quickens them. ''The Son quickeneth whom he will'' (John 5:21). It is Christ who washes away their sins. He has ''loved us, and washed us from our sins in his own blood'' (Rev. 1:5). It is Christ who gives them peace. ''Peace I leave with you, my peace I give unto you'' (John 14:27). It is Christ who gives them eternal life. ''I give unto them eternal life; and they shall never perish'' (John 10:28). It is Christ who grants them repentance. ''Him hath God exalted to be a Prince and a Saviour, to give repentance'' (Acts 5:31). It is Christ who enables them to become God's children. ''To as many as received him, to them gave he power to become the sons of God'' (John 1:12). It is Christ who carries on the work within them when it is begun. ''Because I live, ye shall live also'' (John 14:19). In short, it has ''pleased the Father that in Christ should all fulness dwell'' (Col. 1:19). He is the author and finisher of faith. He is the life. He is the head. From Him every joint and member of the mystical body of Christians is supplied. Through Him they are strengthened for duty. By Him they are kept from falling. He shall preserve

them to the end, and present them faultless before the
Father's throne with exceeding great joy. He is all things
in all believers.

The mighty agent by whom the Lord Jesus Christ carries out this work in the members of His church, is, without doubt, the Holy Ghost. He it is who applies Christ
and His benefits to the soul. He it is who is ever renewing, awakening, convincing, leading to the cross, transforming, taking out of the world stone after stone, and
adding it to the mystical building. But the great chief
Builder, who has undertaken to execute the work of
redemption and bring it to completion, is the Son of
God, the "Word who was made flesh." It is Jesus Christ
who "builds."

In building the true church, the Lord Jesus conde-
scends to use many subordinate instruments. The ministry of the gospel, the circulation of the Scriptures, the
friendly rebuke, the word spoken in season, the drawing
influence of afflictions—all, all are means and appli-
ances by which His work is carried on, and the Spirit conveys life to souls. But Christ is the great superintending
architect, ordering, guiding, directing all that is done.
Paul may plant, and Apollos water, but God giveth the
increase (I Cor. 3:6). Ministers may preach, and writers
may write, but the Lord Jesus Christ alone can build.
And except He builds, the work stands still.

Great is the *wisdom* wherewith the Lord Jesus Christ
builds His church! All is done at the right time, and in
the right way. Each stone in its turn is put in its right
place. Sometimes He chooses great stones, and sometimes He chooses small stones. Sometimes the work goes
on fast, and sometimes it goes on slowly. Man is frequently impatient, and thinks that nothing is doing.
But man's time is not God's time. A thousand years in
His sight are but as a single day. The great Builder makes

no mistakes. He knows what He is doing. He sees the end from the beginning. He works by a perfect, unalterable, and certain plan. The mightiest conceptions of architects, like Michelangelo and Wren, are mere trifling and child's play, in comparison with Christ's wise counsels respecting His church.

Great is the *condescension and mercy* which Christ exhibits in building His church! He often chooses the most unlikely and roughest stones, and fits them into a most excellent work. He despises none, and rejects none, on account of former sins and past transgressions. He often makes Pharisees and publicans become pillars of His house. He delights to show mercy. He often takes the most thoughtless and ungodly, and transforms them into polished corners of His spiritual temple.

Great is the *power* which Christ displays in building His church! He carries on His work in spite of opposition from the world, the flesh, and the devil. In storm, in tempest, through troublous times, silently, quietly, without noise, without stir, without excitement, the building progresses, like Solomon's temple. "I will work," He declares, "and who shall let it?" (Isa. 43:13).

The children of this world take little or no interest in the building of this church. They care nothing for the conversion of souls. What are broken spirits and penitent hearts to them? What is conviction of sin, or faith in the Lord Jesus to them? It is all "foolishness" in their eyes. But while the children of this world care nothing, there is joy in the presence of the angels of God. For the preserving of the true church, the laws of nature have oftentimes been suspended. For the good of that church, all the providential dealings of God in this world are ordered and arranged. For the elect's sake, wars are brought to an end, and peace is given to a nation. Statesmen, rulers, emperors, kings, presidents, heads of governments, have their schemes and plans, and think them of vast importance. But there is another work going on of infinitely greater moment, for which they are only the "axes and saws" in God's hands (Isa. 10:15). That work is the erection of Christ's spiritual temple, the gathering in of living stones into the one true church.

We ought to feel deeply thankful that the building of the true church is laid on the shoulders of one that is mighty. If the work depended on man, it would soon stand still. But, blessed be God, the work is in the hands of a builder who never fails to accomplish His designs! Christ is the almighty Builder. He will carry on His work, though nations and visible churches may not know their duty. Christ will never fail. That which He has undertaken He will certainly accomplish.

III. I pass on to the third point, which I proposed to consider, the *Foundation* upon which this church is built. The Lord Jesus Christ tells us, "Upon this rock will I build my church."

What did the Lord Jesus Christ mean, when He spoke of this foundation? Did He mean the apostle Peter, to whom He was speaking? I think assuredly not. I can see no reason, if He meant Peter, why He did not say, "Upon thee" will I build my church. If He had meant Peter, He would surely have said, I will build my church on thee, as plainly as He said, "to thee will I give the keys." No, it was not the person of the apostle Peter, but the good confession which the apostle had just made! It was not Peter, the erring, unstable man, but the mighty truth which the Father had revealed to Peter. It was the truth concerning Jesus Christ Himself which was the rock. It was Christ's mediatorship, and Christ's messiahship. It was the blessed truth, that Jesus was the promised Savior, the true surety, the real intercessor between God and man. This was the rock, and this the foundation, upon which the church of Christ was to be built.

The foundation of the true church was laid at a mighty cost. It needed that the Son of God should take our nature upon Him, and in that nature live, suffer, and die, not for His own sins, but for ours. It needed that in that nature Christ should go to the grave, and rise again. It needed that in that nature Christ should go up to heaven, to sit at the right hand of God, having obtained eternal redemption for all His people. No other foundation could have met the necessities of lost, guilty, corrupt, weak, helpless sinners.

That foundation, once obtained, is very strong. It can bear the weight of the sins of the world. It has borne the weight of all the sins of all the believers who have built on it. Sins of thought, sins of the imagination, sins of the heart, sins of the head, sins which every one has seen, and sins which no man knows, sins against God, and sins against man, sins of all kinds and descriptions—that mighty rock can bear the weight of all these sins, and not give way. The mediatorial office of Christ is a remedy sufficient for all the sins of all the world.

To this one foundation every member of Christ's true church is joined. In many things believers are disunited and disagreed. In the matter of their soul's foundation they are all of one mind. Whether Episcopalians or Presbyterians, Baptists or Methodists, believers all meet at one point. They are all built on the rock. Ask where they get their peace, and hope, and joyful expectation of good things to come. You will find that all flows from that one mighty source, Christ the mediator between God and man, and the office that Christ holds, as the High Priest and surety of sinners.

Look to your foundation, if you would know whether or not you are a member of the one true church. It is a point that may be known to yourself. Your public worship we can see; but we cannot see whether you are personally built upon the rock. Your attendance at the Lord's Table we can see; but we cannot see whether you are joined to Christ, and one with Christ, and Christ in you. Take heed that you make no mistake about your own personal salvation. See that your own soul is upon the rock. Without this, all else is nothing. Without this, you will never stand in the day of judgment. Better a thousand times in that day to be found in a cottage "upon the rock," than in a palace upon the sand!

IV. I proceed in the fourth place to speak of the *Implied Trials* of the church, to which our text refers. There is mention made of "the gates of hell." By that expression we are meant to understand the power of the prince of hell, even the devil (cf. Ps. 9:13; 108:18; Isa. 38:10).

The history of Christ's true church has always been one of conflict and war. It has been constantly assailed by a deadly enemy, Satan, the prince of this world. The devil hates the true church of Christ with an undying hatred. He is ever stirring up opposition against all its members. He is ever urging the children of this world to do his will, and to injure and harass the people of God. If he cannot bruise the head, he will bruise the heel. If he cannot rob believers of heaven, he will vex them by the way.

Warfare with the powers of hell has been the experience of the whole body of Christ for six thousand years. It has always been a bush burning, though not consumed, a woman fleeing into the wilderness, but not swallowed up (Exod. 3:2; Rev. 12:6, 16). The visible churches have their times of prosperity and seasons of peace, but never has there been a time of peace for the true church. Its conflict is perpetual. Its battle never ends.

Warfare with the powers of hell is the experience of every individual member of the true church. Each has to fight. What are the lives of all the saints, but records of battles? What were such men as Paul, and James, and Peter, and John, and Polycarp, and Chrysostom, and Augustine, and Luther, and Calvin, and Latimer, and Baxter, but soldiers engaged in a constant warfare? Sometimes the persons of the saints have been assailed, and sometimes their property. Sometimes they have been harassed by calumnies and slanders, and sometimes by open persecution. But in one way or another the devil has been continually warring against the church. The "gates of hell" have been continually assaulting the people of Christ.

We who preach the gospel can hold out to all who come to Christ, "exceeding great and precious promises" (II Peter 1:4). We can offer boldly to you, in our Master's name, the peace of God which passeth all understanding. Mercy, free grace, and full salvation, are offered to every one who will come to Christ, and believe on Him. But we promise you no peace with the world, or with the devil. We warn you, on the contrary, that there must be warfare, so long as you are in the body. We would not keep you back, or deter you from Christ's service. But we would have you "count the cost," and fully understand what Christ's service entails (Luke 14:28).

(a) Marvel not at the enmity of the gates of hell. "If ye were of the world, the world would love his own" (John 15:19). So long as the world is the world, and the

devil the devil, so long there must be warfare, and
believers in Christ must be soldiers. The world hated
Christ, and the world will hate true Christians, as long as
the earth stands. As the great reformer, Luther, said,
"Cain will go on murdering Abel so long as the Church
is on earth."

(b) Be prepared for the enmity of the gates of hell.
Put on the whole armor of God. The tower of David contains a thousand bucklers, all ready for the use of God's
people. The weapons of our warfare have been tried by
millions of poor sinners like ourselves, and have never
been found to fail.

(c) Be patient under the enmity of the gates of hell. It
is all working together for your good. It tends to sanctify. It will keep you awake. It will make you humble. It
will drive you nearer to the Lord Jesus Christ. It will
wean you from the world. It will help to make you pray
more. Above all, it will make you long for heaven. It will
teach you to say with heart as well as lips, "Come, Lord
Jesus. Thy kingdom come."

(d) Be not cast down by the enmity of hell. The warfare of the true child of God is as much a mark of grace as
the inward peace which he enjoys. No cross, no crown!
No conflict, no saving Christianity! "Blessed are ye,"
said our Lord Jesus Christ, "when men shall revile you,
and persecute you, and shall say all manner of evil
against you falsely, for my sake." If you are never persecuted for religion's sake, and all men speak well of you,
you may well doubt whether you belong to "the church
on the rock" (Matt. 5:11; Luke 6:26).

V. There remains one thing more to be considered,
the *Security* of the true church of Christ. There is a glorious promise given by the Builder, "The gates of hell
shall not prevail."

He who cannot lie has pledged His word, that all the powers of hell shall never overthrow His church. It shall continue, and stand, in spite of every assault. It shall never be overcome. All other created things perish and pass away, but not the church which is built on the rock.

Empires have risen and fallen in rapid succession. Egypt, Assyria, Babylon, Persia, Tyre, Carthage, Rome, Greece, Venice—Where are all these now? They were all the creations of man's hand, and have passed away. But the true church of Christ lives on.

The mightiest cities have become heaps of ruins. The broad walls of Babylon have sunk to the ground. The palaces of Nineveh are covered with mounds of dust. The hundred gates of Thebes are only matters of history. Tyre is a place where fishermen hang their nets. Carthage is a desolation. Yet all this time the true church stands. The gates of hell do not prevail against it.

The earliest visible churches have in many cases decayed and perished. Where is the Church of Ephesus and the Church of Antioch? Where is the Church of Alexandria and the Church of Constantinople? Where are the Corinthian, and Philippian, and Thessalonian churches? Where, indeed, are they all? They departed from the Word of God. They were proud of their bishops, and synods, and ceremonies, and learning, and antiquity. They did not glory in the true cross of Christ. They did not hold fast the gospel. They did not give the Lord Jesus His rightful office, or faith its rightful place. They are now among the things that have been. Their candlestick has been taken away. But all this time the true church has lived on.

Has the true church been oppressed in one country? It has fled to another. Has it been trampled on and oppressed in one soil? It has taken root and flourished in some other climate. Fire, sword, prisons, fines, penalties, have never been able to destroy its vitality. Its persecutors have died and gone to their own place, but the Word of God has lived, and grown, and multiplied. Weak as this true church may appear to the eye of man, it is an anvil which has broken many a hammer in times past, and perhaps will break many more before the end. "He that lays hands on it, is touching the apple of his eye" (Zech. 2:8).

The promise of our text is true of the *whole body* of the true church. Christ will never be without a witness in the world. He has had a people in the worst of times. He had seven thousand in Israel even in the days of Ahab. There are some now, I believe, in the dark places of the Roman and Greek churches, who, in spite of much weakness, are serving Christ. The devil may rage horribly. The church in some countries may be brought exceedingly low. But the gates of hell shall never entirely "prevail."

The promise of our text is true of *every individual* member of the church. Some of God's people have been so much cast down and disquieted, that they have despaired of their safety. Some have fallen sadly, as David and Peter did. Some have departed from the faith for a time, like Cranmer and Jewell. Many have been tried by cruel doubts and fears. But all have got safe home at last, the youngest as well as the oldest, the weakest as well as the strongest. And so it will be to the end. Can you prevent tomorrow's sun from rising? Can you prevent the tide in the Bristol Channel from ebbing and flowing? Can you prevent the planets moving in their respective orbits? Then, and then alone, can you prevent the salvation of any believer, however feeble, the final safety of any living stone in that church which is built upon the rock, however small or insignificant that stone may appear.

The true church is Christ's body. Not one bone in that mystical body shall ever be broken. The true church is Christ's bride. Those whom God hath joined in everlasting covenant, shall never be put asunder. The true church is Christ's flock. When the lion came and took a lamb out of David's flock, David arose and delivered the lamb from his mouth. Christ will do the same. He is David's greater son. Not a single sick lamb in Christ's flock shall perish. He will say to His Father in the last day, "Of them which thou gavest me have I lost none" (John 18:9). The true church is the wheat of the earth. It may be sifted, winnowed, buffeted, tossed to and fro. But not one grain shall be lost. The tares and chaff shall be burned. The wheat shall be gathered into the barn. The true church is Christ's army. The Captain of our salvation loses none of His soldiers. His plans are never defeated. His supplies never fail. His muster-roll is the same at the end as it was at the beginning. Of the men that marched gallantly out of England a few years ago in the Crimean war, how many never came back! Regiments that went forth, strong and cheerful, with bands playing and banners flying, laid their bones in a foreign land, and never returned to their native country. But it is not so with Christ's army. Not one of His soldiers shall be missing at last. He Himself declares, "They shall never perish" (John 10:28).

The devil may cast some of the members of the true church into prison. He may kill, and burn, and torture, and hang. But after he has killed the body, there is nothing more that he can do. He cannot hurt the soul. When the French troops took Rome a few years ago, they found on the walls of a prison cell, under the Inquisition, the words of a prisoner. Who he was, we know not. But his words are worthy of remembrance. "Though dead, he yet speaketh." He had written on the walls, very likely after an unjust trial, and a still more unjust excommunication, the following striking words: "Blessed Jesus, they cannot cast me out of Thy true Church." That record is true! Not all the power of Satan can cast out of Christ's true church one single believer.

I trust that no reader of this paper will ever allow fear to prevent his beginning to serve Christ. He to whom you commit your soul has all power in heaven and earth, and He will keep you. He will never let you be cast away. Relatives may oppose. Neighbors may mock. The world may slander, and ridicule, and jest, and sneer. Fear not! Fear not! The powers of hell shall never prevail against your soul. Greater is He that is for you, than all they that are against you.

Fear not for the church of Christ, when ministers die, and saints are taken away. Christ can ever maintain His own cause. He will raise up better servants and brighter stars. The stars are all in His right hand. Leave off all anxious thought about the future. Cease to be cast down by the measures of statesmen, or the plots of wolves in sheep's clothing. Christ will ever provide for His own church. Christ will take care that "The gates of hell shall not prevail against it." All is going on well, though our eyes may not see it. The kingdoms of this world shall yet become the kingdoms of our God, and of His Christ.

I will now conclude this paper with a few words of practical application.

(1) My first word of application shall be *a question*. What shall that question be? What shall I ask? I will return to the point with which I began. I will go back to the first sentence with which I opened my paper. I ask you, whether you are a member of the one true church of Christ? Are you in the highest, the best sense, a "churchman" in the sight of God? You know now what I mean. I look far beyond the Church of England. I am

not speaking of church or chapel. I speak of "the church built upon the rock." I ask you, with all solemnity, Are you a member of that church? Are you joined to the great foundation? Are you on the rock? Have you received the Holy Ghost? Does the Spirit witness with your spirit, that you are one with Christ, and Christ with you? I beseech you, in the name of God, to lay to heart these questions, and to ponder them well. If you are not converted, you do not yet belong to the "church on the rock."

Let every reader of this paper take heed to himself, if he cannot give a satisfactory answer to my inquiry. Take heed, take heed that you do not make shipwreck of your soul to all eternity. Take heed, lest at last the gates of hell prevail against you, the devil claim you as his own, and you be cast away forever. Take heed, lest you go down to the pit from the land of Bibles, and in the full light of Christ's gospel. Take heed, lest you are found at the left hand of Christ at last—a lost Episcopalian or a lost Presbyterian, a lost Baptist or a lost Methodist—lost because, with all your zeal for your own party and your own communion table, you never joined the one true church.

(2) My second work of application shall be *an invitation*. I address it to every one who is not yet a true believer. I say to you, come and join the one true church without delay. Come and join yourself to the Lord Jesus Christ in an everlasting covenant not to be forgotten.

Consider well what I say. I charge you solemnly not to mistake the meaning of my invitation. I do not bid you leave the visible church to which you belong. I abhor all idolatry of forms and parties. I detest a proselytizing spirit. But I do bid you come to Christ and be saved. The day of decision must come some time. Why not this very hour? Why not today, while it is called today? Why not this very night, ere the sun rises tomorrow morning? Come to Him, who died for sinners on the cross, and invites all sinners to come to Him by faith and be saved. Come to my Master, Jesus Christ. Come, I say, for all things are now ready. Mercy is ready for you. Heaven is ready for you. Angels are ready to rejoice over you. Christ is ready to receive you. Christ will receive you gladly, and welcome you among His children. Come into the ark. The flood of God's wrath will soon break upon the earth; come into the ark and be safe.

Come into the lifeboat of the one true church. This old world will soon break into pieces! Hear you not the tremblings of it? The world is but a wreck hard upon the sandbank. The night is far-spent, the waves are beginning to rise, the wind is getting up, the storm will soon shatter the old wreck. But the lifeboat is launched, and we, the ministers of the gospel, beseech you to come into the lifeboat and be saved. We beseech you to arise at once and come to Christ.

Dost thou ask, "How can I come? My sins are too many. I am too wicked yet. I dare not come." Away with the thought! It is a temptation of Satan. Come to Christ as a sinner. Come just as you are. Hear the words of that beautiful hymn:

> Just as I am, without one plea,
> But that Thy blood was shed for me,
> And that Thou bid'st me come to Thee,
>   O Lamb of God I come.

This is the way to come to Christ. You should come, waiting for nothing, and tarrying for nothing. You should come, as a hungry sinner, to be filled; as a poor sinner, to be enriched; as a bad, undeserving sinner, to be clothed with righteousness. So coming, Christ would receive you. "Him that cometh" to Christ, He "will in no wise cast out." Oh, come, come to Jesus Christ. Come into "the true church" by faith and be saved.

(3) Last of all, let me give a word of *exhortation* to all believers into whose hands this paper may fall.

Strive to live a *holy* life. Walk worthy of the church to which you belong. Live like citizens of heaven. Let your light shine before men, so that the world may profit by your conduct. Let them know whose you are, and whom you serve. Be epistles of Christ, known and read of all men, written in such clear letters, that none can say of you, "I know not whether this man be a member of Christ or not." He that knows nothing of real, practical holiness is no member of "the church on the rock."

Strive to live a *courageous* life. Confess Christ before men. Whatever station you occupy, in that station confess Christ. Why should you be ashamed of Him? He was not ashamed of you on the cross. He is ready to confess you now before His Father in heaven. Why should you be ashamed of Him? Be bold. Be very bold. The good soldier is not ashamed of his uniform. The true believer ought never to be ashamed of Christ.

Strive to live a *joyful* life. Live like men who look for that blessed hope—the second coming of Jesus Christ. This is the prospect to which we should all look forward. It is not so much the thought of going to heaven, as of heaven coming to us, that should fill our minds. "There is a good time coming" for all the people of God, a good time for all the church of Christ, a good time for all believers; a bad time for the impenitent and unbelieving, but a good time for true Christians. For that good time, let us wait, and watch, and pray.

The scaffolding will soon be taken down. The last stone will soon be brought out. The topstone will be placed upon the edifice. Yet a little time, and the full beauty of the church which Christ is building shall be clearly seen.

The great Master Builder will soon come Himself. A building shall be shown to assembled worlds, in which there shall be no imperfection. The Savior and the saved shall rejoice together. The whole universe shall acknowledge, that in the building of Christ's church all was well done. "Blessed"—it shall be said in that day, if it was never said before—"BLESSED ARE ALL THEY WHO BELONG TO THE CHURCH ON THE ROCK!"

8
The Family of God

"The whole family in heaven and earth."—
Eph. 3:15

The words which form the title of this paper
ought to stir some feelings in our minds at any time.
There lives not the man or woman on earth who is not
member of some "family." The poorest as well as the
richest has his kith and kin, and can tell you something
of his "family."

Family gatherings at certain times of the year, such as
Christmas, we all know, are very common. Thousands of
firesides are crowded then, if at no other time of the
year. The young man in town snatches a few days from
business, and takes a run down to the old folks at home.
The young woman in service gets a short holiday, and
comes to visit her father and mother. Brothers and sisters
meet for a few hours. Parents and children look one another in the face. How much there is to talk about! How
many questions to be asked! How many interesting
things to be told! Happy indeed is that fireside which
sees gathered round it at Christmas "the whole family"!

Family gatherings are natural, and right, and good. I
approve them with all my heart. It does me good to see

them kept up. They are one of the very few pleasant things which have survived the fall of man. Next to the grace of God, I see no principle which unites people so much in this sinful world as family feeling. Community of blood is a most powerful tie. It was a fine saying of an American naval officer, when his men insisted on helping the English sailors in fighting the Taku forts in China, "I cannot help it: blood is thicker than water." I have often observed that people will stand up for their relations, merely because they *are* their relations, and refuse to hear a word against them, even when they have no sympathy with their tastes and ways. Anything which helps to keep up family feeling ought to be commended. It is a wise thing, when it can be done, to gather together at Christmas "the whole family."

Family gatherings, nevertheless, are often sorrowful things. It would be strange indeed, in such a world as this, if they were not. Few are the family circles which do not show gaps and vacant places as years pass away. Changes and deaths made sad havoc as time goes on. Thoughts will rise up within us, as we grow older, about faces and voices no longer with us, which no Christmas merriment can entirely keep down. When the young members of the family have once begun to launch forth into the world, the old heads may long survive the scattering of the nest; but after a certain time, it seldom happens that you see together "the whole family."

There is one great family to which I want all the readers of this paper to belong. It is a family despised by many, and not even known by some. But it is a family of far more importance than any family on earth. To belong to it entitles a man to far greater privileges than to be the son of a king. It is the family of which St. Paul speaks to the Ephesians, when he tells them of the "whole family in heaven and earth." It is the family of God.

I ask the attention of every reader of this paper while I try to describe this family, and recommend it to his notice. I want to tell you of the amazing benefits which membership of this family conveys. I want you to be found one of this family, when its gathering shall come at last—a gathering without separation, or sorrow, or tears. Hear me while, as a minister of Christ, and friend to your soul, I speak to you for a few minutes about "the whole family in heaven and earth."

I. First of all, *what is this family?*

II. Secondly, *what is its present position?*

III. Thirdly, *what are its future prospects?*

I wish to unfold these three things before you, and I invite your serious consideration of them. Our family gatherings on earth must have an end one day. Our last earthly Christmas must come. Happy indeed is that Christmas which finds us prepared to meet God!

I. *What is that family* which the Bible calls "the whole family in heaven and earth"? Of whom does it consist?

The family before us consists of all real Christians, of all who have the Spirit, of all true believers in Christ, of the saints of every age, and church, and nation, and tongue. It includes the blessed company of all faithful people. It is the same as the election of God, the household of faith, the mystical body of Christ, the bride, the living temple, the sheep that never perish, the church of the first-born, the holy Catholic Church. All these expressions are only "the family of God" under other names.

Membership of the family before us does not depend on any earthly connection. It comes not by natural birth, but by new birth. Ministers cannot impart it to their hearers. Parents cannot give it to their children. You may be born in the godliest family in the land, and enjoy the richest means of grace a church can supply, and yet never belong to the family of God. To belong to it you must be born again. None but the Holy Ghost can make a living member of His family. It is His special office and prerogative to bring into the true church such as shall be saved. They that are born again are born, "not of blood, nor of the will of the flesh, nor of the will of man, but of God" (John 1:13).

Do you ask the reason of this name which the Bible gives to the company of all true Christians? Would you like to know why they are called "a family"? Listen and I will tell you.

(a) True Christians are called "a family" because they have all *one Father*. They are all children of God by faith in Christ Jesus. They are all born of one Spirit. They are all sons and daughters of the Lord almighty. They have received the Spirit of adoption, whereby they cry, Abba, Father (Gal. 3:26; John 3:8; II Cor. 6:18; Rom. 8:15). They do not regard God with slavish fear, as an austere being, only ready to punish them. They look up to Him with tender confidence, as a reconciled and loving parent, as one forgiving iniquity, transgression, and sin, to all who believe on Jesus, and full of pity even to the least and feeblest. The words, "Our Father which art in heaven," are no mere form in the mouth of true Christians. No wonder they are called God's "family."

(b) True Christians are called "a family," because they all *rejoice in one name*. That name is the name of their great head and elder brother, even Jesus Christ the Lord. Just as a common family name is the uniting link to all the members of a Highland clan, so does the name of Jesus tie all believers together in one vast family. As members of outward visible churches they have various names and distinguishing appellations. As living members of Christ, they all, with one heart and mind, rejoice in one Savior. Not a heart among them but feels drawn to Jesus as the only object of hope. Not a tongue among them but would tell you that "Christ is all." Sweet to them all is the thought of Christ's death for them on the cross. Sweet is the thought of Christ's intercession for them at the right hand of God. Sweet is the thought of Christ's coming again to unite them to Himself in one glorified company forever. In fact, you might as well take away the sun out of heaven, as take away the name of Christ from believers. To the world there may seem little in His name. To believers it is full of comfort, hope, joy, rest, and peace. No wonder they are called "a family."

(c) True Christians, above all, are called "a family" because there is so strong *a family likeness* among them. They are all led by one Spirit, and are marked by the same general features of life, heart, taste, and character. Just as there is a general bodily resemblance among the brothers and sisters of a family, so there is a general spiritual resemblance among all the sons and daughters of the Lord almighty. They all hate sin and love God. They all rest their hope of salvation on Christ, and have no confidence in themselves. They all endeavor to "come out and be separate" from the ways of the world, and to set their affections on things above. They all turn naturally to the same Bible, as the only food of their souls and the only sure guide in their pilgrimage toward heaven: they find it a "lamp to their feet, and a light to their path" (Ps. 119:105). They all go to the same throne of grace in prayer, and find it as needful to speak to God as to breathe. They all live by the same rule, the Word of God, and strive to conform their daily life to its precepts. They have all the same inward experience. Repentance, faith, hope, charity, humility, inward conflict, are things with which they are all more or less acquainted. No wonder they are called "a family."

This family likeness among true believers is a thing that deserves special attention. To my own mind it is one of the strongest indirect evidences of the truth of Christianity. It is one of the greatest proofs of the reality of the work of the Holy Ghost. Some true Christians live in civilized countries, and some in the midst of heathen lands. Some are highly educated, and some are unable to read a letter. Some are rich and some are poor. Some are churchmen and some are dissenters. Some are old and some are young. And yet, notwithstanding all this, there is a marvelous oneness of heart and character among them. Their joys and their sorrows, their love and their hatred, their likes and their dislikes, their tastes and their distastes, their hopes and their fears, are all most curiously alike. Let others think what they please, I see in all this the finger of God. His handiwork is always one and the same. No wonder that true Christians are compared to "a family."

Take a converted Englishman and a converted Hindu, and let them suddenly meet for the first time. I will engage, if they can understand one another's language, they will soon find common ground between them, and feel at home. The one may have been brought up at Eton and Oxford, and enjoyed every privilege of English civilization. The other may have been trained in the midst of gross heathenism, and accustomed to habits, ways, and manners as unlike the Englishman's as darkness compared to light. And yet now in half an hour they feel that they are friends! The Englishman finds that he has more in common with his Hindu brother than he has with many an old college companion or school-fellow! Who can account for this? How can it be explained? Nothing can account for it but the unity of the Spirit's teaching. It is "one touch" of grace (not nature) "that makes the whole world kin." God's people are in the highest sense "a family."

This is the family to which I wish to direct the attention of my readers in this paper. This is the family to which I want you to belong. I ask you this day to consider it well, if you never considered it before. I have shown you the Father of the family—the God and Father of our Lord Jesus Christ. I have shown you the head and elder brother of the family—the Lord Jesus Himself. I have shown you the features and characteristics of the family. Its members have all great marks of resemblance. Once more I say, consider it well.

Outside this family, remember, there is no salvation. None but those who belong to it, according to the Bible, are in the way that leads to heaven. The salvation of our souls does not depend on union with one church or separation from another. They are miserably deceived who think that it does, and will find it out to their cost one day, except they awake. No, the life of our souls depends on something far more important. This is life eternal, to be a member of "the whole family in heaven and earth."

II. I will now pass on to the second thing which I promised to consider. *What is the present position* of the whole family in heaven and earth?

The family to which I am directing the attention of my readers this day is divided into two great parts. Each part has its own residence or dwelling-place. Part of the family is in heaven, and part is on earth. For the present the two parts are entirely separated from one another. But they form one body in the sight of God, though resident in two places; and their union is sure to take place one day.

Two places, be it remembered, and two only, contain the family of God. The Bible tells us of no third habitation. There is no such thing as purgatory, whatever some Christians may think fit to say. There is no house of purifying, training, or probation for those who are not true Christians when they die. Oh no! There are but two parts of the family—the part that is seen and the part that is unseen, the part that is in "heaven" and the part that is on "earth." The members of the family that are not in heaven are on earth, and those that are not on earth are in heaven. Two parts, and two only! Two places, and two only! Let this never be forgotten.

Some of God's family are safe *in heaven*. They are at rest in that place which the Lord Jesus expressly calls "paradise" (Luke 23:43). They have finished their course. They have fought their battle. They have done their appointed work. They have learned their lessons. They have carried their cross. They have passed through the waves of this troublesome world, and reached the harbor. Little as we know about them, we know that they are happy. They are no longer troubled by sin and temptation. They have said good-bye forever to poverty and anxiety, to pain and sickness, to sorrow and tears. They are with Christ Himself, who loved them and gave Himself for them, and in His company they must needs be happy (Phil. 1:23). They have nothing to fear in looking back to the past. They have nothing to dread in looking forward to things to come. Three things only are lacking to make their happiness complete. These three are the second advent of Christ in glory, the resurrection of their own bodies, and the gathering together of all believers. And of these three things they are sure.

Some of God's family are still *upon earth*. They are scattered to and fro in the midst of a wicked world, a few in one place and a few in another. All are more or less occupied in the same way, according to the measure of their grace. All are running a race, doing a work, warring a warfare, carrying a cross, striving against sin, resisting the devil, crucifying the flesh, struggling against the world, witnessing for Christ, mourning over their own hearts, hearing, reading, and praying, however feebly, for the life of their souls. Each is often disposed to think no cross so heavy as his own, no work so difficult, no heart so hard. But each and all hold on their way—a wonder to the ignorant world around them, and often a wonder to themselves.

But, however divided God's family may be at present in dwelling-place and local habitation, it is still one family. Both parts of it are still one in character, one in possessions, and one in relation to God. The part in heaven has not so much superiority over the part on earth as at first sight may appear. The difference between the two is only one of degree.

(a) Both parts of the family love the same Savior, and delight in the same perfect will of God. But the part on earth loves with much imperfection and infirmity, and lives by faith, not by sight. The part in heaven loves without weakness, or doubt, or distraction. It walks by sight and not by faith, and sees what it once believed.

(b) Both parts of the family are saints. But the saints on earth are often poor weary pilgrims, who find the "flesh lusting against the Spirit, and the Spirit lusting against the flesh, so that they cannot do the things they would" (Gal. 5:17). They live in the midst of an evil world, and are often sick of themselves and of the sin they see around them. The saints in heaven, on the con-

trary, are delivered from the world, the flesh, and the devil, and enjoy a glorious liberty. They are called "the spirits of just men made perfect" (Heb. 12:23).

(c) Both parts of the family are alike God's children. But the children in heaven have learned all their lessons, have finished their appointed tasks, have begun an eternal holiday. The children on earth are still at school. They are daily learning wisdom, though slowly and with much trouble, and often needing to be reminded of their past lessons by chastisement and the rod. Their holidays are yet to come.

(d) Both parts of the family are alike God's soldiers. But the soldiers on earth are yet militant. Their warfare is not accomplished. Their fight is not over. They need every day to put on the whole armor of God. The soldiers in heaven are all triumphant. No enemy can hurt them now. No fiery dart can reach them. Helmet and shield may both be laid aside. They may at last say to the sword of the Spirit, "Rest and be still." They may at length sit down, and need not to watch and stand on their guard.

(e) Last, but not least, both parts of the family are alike safe and secure. Wonderful as this may sound, it is true. Christ cares as much for His members on earth as His members in heaven. You might as well think to pluck the stars out of heaven, as to pluck one saint, however feeble, out of Christ's hand. Both parts of the family are alike secured by "an everlasting covenant, ordered in all things, and sure" (II Sam. 23:5). The members on earth, through the burden of the flesh and the dimness of their faith, may neither see, nor know, nor feel their own safety. But they are safe, though they may not see it. The whole family is "kept by the power of God through faith unto salvation" (I Peter 1:5). The members yet on the road are as secure as the members who have got home. Not one shall be found missing at the last day. The words of the Christian poet shall be found strictly true:

> More happy, but not more secure,
> The glorified spirits in heaven.

Before I leave this part of my subject, I ask every reader of this paper to understand thoroughly the present position of God's family, and to form a just estimate of it. Learn not to measure its numbers or its privileges by what you see with your eyes. You see only a small body of believers in this present time. But you must not forget that a great company has got safe to heaven already, and that when all are assembled at the last day they will be "a multitude, which no man could number" (Rev. 7:9). You only see that part of the family which is struggling on earth. You must never forget that the greater part of the family has got home and is resting in heaven. You see the militant part, but not the triumphant. You see the part that is carrying the cross, but not the part which is safe in paradise. The family of God is far more rich and glorious than you suppose. Believe me, it is no small thing to belong to the "whole family in heaven and earth."

III. I will now pass on to the last thing which I promised to consider. *What are the future prospects of* the whole family in heaven and earth?

The future prospects of a family! What a vast amount of uncertainty these words open up when we look at any family now in the world! How little we can tell of the things coming on any of us! What a mercy that we do not know the sorrows and trials and separations through which our beloved children may have to pass, when we have left the world! It is a mercy that we do not know "what a day may bring forth," and a far greater mercy that we do not know what may happen in twenty years (Prov. 27:1). Alas, foreknowledge of the future prospects of our belongings would spoil many a family gathering, and fill the whole party with gloom!

Think how many a fine boy, who is now the delight of his parents, will by and by walk in the prodigal's footsteps, and never return home! Think how many a fair daughter, the joy of a mother's heart, will follow the bent of her self-will after a few years, and insist on some miserably mistaken marriage! Think how disease and pain will often lay low the loveliest of a family circle, and make her life a burden and weariness to herself, if not to others! Think of the endless breaches and divisions arising out of money matters! Alas, there is many a lifelong quarrel about a few pounds, between those who once played together in the same nursery! Think of these things. The "future prospects" of many a family which meets together every Christmas are a solemn and serious subject. Hundreds, to say the least, are gathering together for the last time: when they part, they will never meet again.

But, thank God, there is one great family whose "prospects" are very different. It is the family of which I am speaking in this paper, and commending to your attention. The future prospects of the family of God are not uncertain. They are good, and only good—happy, and only happy. Listen to me, and I will try to set them in order before you.

(a) The members of God's family shall all be *brought safe home* one day. Here upon earth they may be scattered, tried, tossed with tempests, and bowed down with afflictions. But not one of them shall perish (John 10:28). The weakest lamb shall not be left to perish in the wilderness; the feeblest child shall not be missing when the muster-roll is brought out at the last day. In spite of the world, the flesh, and the devil, the whole family shall get home. "If, when we were enemies, we were reconciled to God by the death of his Son, much more, being reconciled, we shall be saved by his life" (Rom. 5:10).

(b) The members of God's family *shall all have glorious bodies* one day. When the Lord Jesus Christ comes the second time, the dead saints shall all be raised and the living shall all be changed. They shall no longer have a vile mortal body, full of weaknesses and infirmities: they shall have a body like that of their risen Lord, without the slightest liability to sickness and pain. They shall no longer be clogged and hindered by an aching frame, when they want to serve God: they shall be able to serve Him night and day without weariness, and to attend upon Him without distraction. The former things will have passed away. That word will be fulfilled, "I make all things new" (Rev. 21:5).

(c) The members of God's family shall all be *gathered into one company* one day. It matters nothing where they have lived or where they have died. They may have been separated from one another both by time and space. One may have lived in tents, with Abraham, Isaac, and Jacob, and another traveled by railway in our own day. One may have laid his bones in an Australian desert, and another may have been buried in an English churchyard. It makes no difference. All shall be gathered together from north and south, and east and west, and meet in one happy assembly, to part no more. The earthly partings of God's family are only for a few days. Their meeting is for eternity. It matters little where we live. It is a time of scattering now, and not of gathering. It matters little where we die. All graves are equally near to paradise. But it does matter much whether we belong to God's family. If we do we are sure to meet again at last.

(d) The members of God's family shall all be *united in mind and judgment* one day. They are not so now about many little things. About the things needful to salvation there is a marvelous unity among them. About many speculative points in religion, about forms of worship and church government, they often sadly disagree. But there shall be no disagreement among them one day. Ephraim shall no longer vex Judah, nor Judah Ephraim. Churchmen shall no more quarrel with dissenters, nor dissenters with churchmen. Partial knowledge and dim vision shall be at an end forever. Divisions and separations, misunderstandings and misconstructions, shall be buried and forgotten. As there shall only be one language, so there shall only be one opinion. At last, after six thousand years of strife and jangling, perfect unity and harmony shall be found. A family shall at length be shown to angels and men in which all are of one mind.

(e) The members of God's family shall all be *perfected in holiness* one day. They are not literally perfect now, although "complete in Christ" (Col. 2:10). Though born again, and renewed after the image of Christ, they offend and fall short in many things (James 3:2). None know it better than they do themselves. It is their grief and sorrow that they do not love God more heartily and serve Him more faithfully. But they shall be completely freed from all corruption one day. They shall rise again at Christ's second appearing without any of the infirmities which cleave to them in their lives. Not a single evil temper or corrupt inclination shall be found in them. They shall be presented by their Head to the Father, without spot, or wrinkle, or any such thing, perfectly holy and without blemish, fair as the moon, and clear as the sun (Eph. 5:27; Cant. 5:10). Grace, even now, is a beautiful thing, when it lives, and shines, and flourishes in the midst of imperfection. But how much more beautiful will grace appear when it is seen pure, unmixed, unmingled, and alone! And it shall be seen so when Christ comes to be glorified in His saints at the last day.

(f) Last, but not least, the members of God's family shall all be *eternally provided for* one day. When the affairs of this sinful world are finally wound up and settled, there shall be an everlasting portion for all the sons and daughters of the Lord almighty. Not even the weakest of them shall be overlooked and forgotten. There shall be something for everyone, according to his measure. The smallest vessel of grace, as well as the greatest, shall be filled to the brim with glory. The precise nature of that glory and reward it would be folly to pretend to describe. It is a thing which eye has not seen, nor mind of man conceived. Enough for us to know that each member of God's family, when he awakes up after His Master's likeness, shall be "satisfied" (Ps. 17:15). Enough, above all, to know that their joy, and glory, and reward shall be forever. What they receive in the day of the Lord they will never lose. The inheritance reserved for them, when they come of age, is "incorruptible, undefiled, and fadeth not away" (I Peter 1:4).

These prospects of God's family are great realities. They are not vague shadowy talk of man's invention. They are real true things, and will be seen as such before long. They deserve your serious consideration. Examine them well.

Look round the families of earth with which you are acquainted, the richest, the greatest, the noblest, the happiest. Where will you find one among them all which can show prospects to compare with those of which you have just heard? The earthly riches, in many a case, will be gone in a hundred years hence. The noble blood, in many a case, will not prevent some disgraceful deed staining the family name. The happiness, in many a case, will be found hollow and seeming. Few, indeed, are the homes which have not a secret sorrow, or "a skeleton in the closet." Whether for present possessions or future prospects, there is no family so well off as "the whole family in heaven and earth." Whether you look at what they have now, or will have hereafter, there is no family like the family of God.

My task is done. My paper is drawing to a close. It only remains to close it with a few words of practical application. Give me your attention for the last time. May God bless what I am going to say to the good of your soul!

(1) I ask you a plain question. Take it with you to every family gathering which you join at any season of the year. Take it with you, and amidst all your happiness make time for thinking about it. It is a simple question, but a solemn one—*Do you yet belong to the family of God?*

To the family of God, remember! This is the point of my question. It is no answer to say that you are a Protestant, or a churchman, or a dissenter. I want to hear of something more and better than that. I want you to have some soul-satisfying and soul-saving religion—a religion that will give you peace while you live, and hope when you die. To have such peace and hope you must be something more than a Protestant, or a churchman, or a dissenter. You must belong to "the family of God." Thousands around you do not belong to it, I can well believe. But that is no reason why you should not.

If you do not yet belong to God's family, I invite you this day to join it without delay. Open your eyes to see the value of your soul, the sinfulness of sin, the holiness of God, the danger of your present condition, the absolute necessity of a mighty change. Open your eyes to see these things, and repent this very day. Open your eyes to see the great Head of God's family, even Christ Jesus, waiting to save your soul. See how He has loved you, lived for you, died for you, risen again for you, and obtained complete redemption for you. See how He offers you free, full, immediate pardon, if you will believe in Him. Open your eyes to see these things. Seek Christ at once. Come and believe on Him, and commit your soul to His keeping this very day.

I know nothing of your family or past history. I know not where you go to spend your leisure weeks, or what company you are going to be in. But I am bold to say, that if you join the family of God you will find it the best and happiest family in the world.

(2) If you really belong to the whole family in heaven and earth, count up your privileges, and *learn to be more thankful.* Think what a mercy it is to have something which the world can neither give nor take away, something which makes you independent of sickness or poverty, something which is your own forevermore. The old family fireside will soon be cold and tenantless. The old family gatherings will soon be past and gone forever. The loving faces we now delight to gaze on are rapidly leaving us. The cheerful voices which now welcome us will soon be silent in the grave. But, thank God, if we belong to Christ's family there is a better gathering yet to come. Let us often think of it, and be thankful!

The family gathering of all God's people will make amends for all that their religion now costs them. A meeting where none are missing, a meeting where there are no gaps and empty places, a meeting where there are no tears, a meeting where there is no parting—such a meeting as this is worth a fight and a struggle. And such a meeting is yet to come to "the whole family in heaven and earth."

In the meantime let us strive to live worthy of the family to which we belong. Let us labor to do nothing that may cause our Father's house to be spoken against. Let us endeavor to make our Master's name beautiful by our temper, conduct, and conversation. Let us love as brethren, and abhor all quarrels. Let us behave as if the honor of "the family" depended on our behavior.

So living, by the grace of God, we shall make our calling and election sure, both to ourselves and others. So living, we may hope to have an abundant entrance, and to enter harbor in full sail, whenever we change earth for heaven (II Peter 1:11). So living, we shall recommend our Father's family to others, and perhaps by God's blessing incline them to say, "We will go with you."

9
"Be Zealous"

"It is good to be zealously affected always in a good thing."—Gal. 4:18

There is a subject before your eyes of vast importance. I mean the subject of religious zeal.

It is a subject, like many others in religion, most sadly misunderstood. Many would be ashamed to be thought "zealous." Many are ready to say of zealous people what Festus said of Paul, "They are beside themselves; they are mad" (Acts 26:24).

But it is a subject which no reader of the Bible has any right to pass over. If we make the Bible our rule of faith and practice, we cannot turn away from it. We must look it in the face. What says the apostle Paul to Titus? Christ "gave himself for us, that he might redeem us from all iniquity, and purify unto himself a peculiar people, *zealous* of good works" (Titus 2:14). What says the Lord Jesus to the Laodicean church? "Be *zealous* and repent" (Rev. 3:19).

Reader, I say plainly, I want to plead the cause of zeal in religion. I am not afraid of it. I love it. I admire it. I believe it to be a mighty blessing. I want to strike a blow at the lazy, easy, sleepy Christianity of these latter days, which can see no beauty in zeal, and only uses the word "zealot" as a word of reproach. I want to remind Christians, that "Zealot" was a name given to one of our Lord Jesus Christ's apostles, and to persuade them to be zealous men.

Come now, and give me your attention, while I tell you something about zeal. Listen to me for your own sake, for the sake of the world, for the sake of the church of Christ. Listen to me, and by God's help, I will show you that to be zealous is to be wise.

I. Let me show you, in the first place, *what is zeal in religion*.

II. Let me show you, in the second place, *when a man can be called rightly zealous in religion*.

III. Let me show you, in the third place, *why it is a good thing for a man to be zealous in religion*.

I. First of all, I propose to bring before you this question, "What is *zeal* in religion?"

Zeal in religion is a burning desire to please God, to do His will, and to advance His glory in the world in every possible way. It is a desire which no man feels by nature, which the Spirit puts into the heart of every believer when he is converted; but which some believers feel so much more strongly than others, that they alone deserve to be called zealous men.

This desire is so strong when it really reigns in a man, that it impels him to make any sacrifice, to go through any trouble, to deny himself to any amount, to suffer, to work, to labor, to toil, to spend himself and be spent, and even to die, if only he can please God and honor Christ.

A zealous man in religion is preeminently *a man of one thing*. It is not enough to say that he is earnest, hearty, uncompromising, thoroughgoing, whole-hearted, fervent in spirit. He only sees one thing, he cares for one thing, he lives for one thing, he is swallowed up in one thing, and that one thing is to please God. Whether he lives, or whether he dies, whether he has health, or whether he has sickness, whether he is rich, or whether he is poor, whether he pleases man, or whether he gives offense, whether he is thought wise, or whether he is thought foolish, whether he gets blame, or whether he gets praise, whether he gets honor, or whether he gets shame—for all this the zealous man cares nothing at all. He burns for one thing, and that one thing is to please God, and to advance God's glory. If he is consumed in the very burning, he cares not for it—he is content. He feels that like a lamp, he is made to burn, and if consumed in burning, he has but done the work for which God appointed him. Such a one will always find a sphere for his zeal. If he cannot preach, and work, and give money, he will cry, and sigh, and pray. Yes, if he is only a pauper, on a perpetual bed of sickness, he will make the wheels of sin around him drive heavily, by continually interceding against it. If he cannot fight in the valley with Joshua, he will do the work of Moses, Aaron, and Hur, on the hill. If he is cut off from working himself, he will give the Lord no rest till help is raised up from another quarter, and the work is done. This is what I mean, when I speak of zeal in religion.

You know the habit of mind that makes men great in this world, that makes such men as Alexander the Great, or Julius Caesar, or Oliver Cromwell, or Peter the Great, or Charles XII, or Marlborough, or Napoleon, or Pitt. You know that they were all men of one thing. They threw themselves into one grand pursuit. They cared for nothing else. They put everything else aside. They counted everything else as second-rate, and of subordinate importance, compared to the one thing that they put before their eyes every day they lived. I say that the same habit of mind applied to the service of the Lord Jesus Christ, becomes religious zeal.

You know the habit of mind that makes men great in the sciences of this world, that makes such men as Archimedes, or Sir Isaac Newton, or Galileo, or Ferguson the astronomer, or James Watt. All these were men of one thing. They brought the powers of their minds into one single focus. They cared for nothing else beside. And this was the secret of their success. I say that this same habit consecrated to the service of God, becomes religious zeal.

You know the habit of mind that makes men rich, that makes men amass mighty fortunes, and leave millions behind them. What kind of people were many of the bankers, and merchants, and tradesmen, who have left a name behind them, as men who acquired immense wealth, and became rich from being poor? They were all men that threw themselves entirely into their business. They gave their first attention, their first thoughts, the best of their time, and the best part of their mind, to pushing forward the transactions in which they were engaged. They were men of one thing. Their hearts were not divided. They devoted themselves, body, soul, and mind, to their business. They seemed to live for nothing else. I say that, if you turn that habit of mind to the service of God and His Christ, it makes religious zeal.

Now, reader, this habit of mind, this zeal was *the characteristic of all the apostles*. See for example the apostle Paul. Hear him when he speaks to the Ephesian elders for the last time, "None of these things move me, neither count I my life dear unto myself, so that I might finish my course with joy, and the ministry that I have received of the Lord Jesus, to testify the gospel of the grace of God" (Acts 20:24). Hear him again, when he writes to the Philippians, "This one thing I do; I press toward the mark for the prize of the high calling of God in Christ Jesus" (Phil. 3:13). See him from the day of his conversion, giving up his brilliant prospects, forsaking all for Christ's sake, and going forth to preach that very Jesus whom he had once despised. See him going to and fro throughout the world from that time, through persecution, through oppression, through opposition, through prisons, through bonds, through afflictions, through things next to death itself, up to the very day when he sealed his faith with his blood, and died at Rome, a martyr for that gospel which he had so long proclaimed. This was true religious *zeal*.

This again, was *the characteristic of the early Christians*. They were men "everywhere spoken against." They were driven to worship God in dens and caves of the earth. They often lost everything in the world for their religion's sake. They generally gained nothing but the cross, persecution, shame, and reproach. But they seldom, very seldom, went back. If they could not dispute, at least they could suffer. If they could not convince their adversaries by argument, at any rate they could die, and prove that they themselves were in earnest. Look at Ignatius cheerfully traveling to the place where he was to be devoured by lions, and saying as he went, "Now do I begin to be a disciple of my master, Christ." Hear old Polycarp before the Roman governor, saying boldly when called upon to deny Christ, "Four score and six years have I served Christ, neither hath He ever offended me in anything, and how then can I revile my King?" This was true *zeal*.

This again was *the characteristic of Martin Luther*. He boldly defied the most powerful hierarchy that the world has ever seen. He unveiled its corruptions with an unflinching hand. He preached the long-neglected truth of justification by faith, in spite of anathemas and excommunications, fast and thickly poured upon him.

See him going to the Diet at Worms, and pleading his cause before the emperor, and the legate, and a host of the children of this world. Hear him saying, when men were dissuading him from going, and reminding him of the fate of John Huss, "Though there were a devil under every tile on the roofs of Worms, in the name of the Lord I shall go forward." This was true *zeal*.

This again was *the characteristic of our own English Reformers*. You have it in our first Reformer, Wycliffe, when he rose up on his sick bed, and said to the friars, who wanted him to retract all he had said against the pope, "I shall not die, but live to declare the villanies of the friars." You have it in Cranmer, content to die at the stake rather than deny Christ's gospel, holding forth that hand to be first burned, which in a moment of weakness had signed a recantation, and saying as he held it in the flames, "This unworthy hand!" You have it in old father Latimer, standing boldly on his faggot, at the age of seventy years, and saying to Ridley, "Courage, brother Ridley! We shall light such a candle this day, as, by God's grace, shall never be put out." This was *zeal*.

This again has been *the characteristic of all the greatest missionaries*. You see it in Mrs. Judson, in Carey, in Morrison, in Schwartz, in Williams, in Brainerd, in Elliott. You see it in none more brightly than in Henry Martyn. This was a man who had reached the highest academical honors that Cambridge could bestow. Whatever profession he chose to follow, he had the most dazzling prospects of success. He turned his back upon it all. He chose to preach the gospel to poor benighted heathen. He went forth to an early grave, in a foreign land. He said when he got there, and saw the condition of the people, "I could bear to be torn in pieces, if I could but hear the sobs of penitence, if I could but see the eyes of faith directed to the Redeemer!" This was *zeal*.

But, reader, to look away from all earthly examples—this, remember, is preeminently the characteristic of our Lord and Savior Jesus Christ Himself. Of Him it was written hundreds of years before He came upon earth, that He was "clad with *zeal* as with a cloak," and "the *zeal* of thine house hath even eaten me." And his own words were, "My meat is to do my Father's will, and to finish his work" (Ps. 69:9; Isa. 59:17; John 4:34).

Where shall we begin, if we try to give examples of His zeal? Where should we end, if we once began? Trace all the narratives of His life in the four Gospels. Read all the history of what He was from the beginning of His ministry to the end. Surely if there ever was one who was *all zeal*, it was our great Example, our Head, our High Priest, the great Shepherd of our Profession, the Lord Jesus Christ.

Reader, if these things are so, you should not only beware of running down zeal, but you should also beware of allowing zeal to be run down in your presence. It may be badly directed, and then it becomes a curse; but it may be turned to the highest and best ends, and then it is a mighty blessing. Like fire not well directed, it is a bad master; but like fire also, if well directed, it is one of the best of servants. Listen not to those people who talk of zeal as weakness and enthusiasm. Listen not to those who see no beauty in missions, who laugh at all attempts at the conversion of souls, who call societies for sending the gospel to the world useless, and who look upon city missions, and district visiting, and ragged schools, and open air preaching, as nothing but foolishness and fanaticism. Beware, lest in joining a cry of that kind you condemn the Lord Jesus Christ Himself. Beware, lest you speak against Him who has ''left us an example, that we should follow his steps'' (I Peter 2:21).

Alas, I fear there are many professing Christians who if they had lived in the days when our Lord and His apostles walked upon earth, would have called Him and all His followers enthusiasts and fanatics! There are many, I fear, who have more in common with Annas and Caiaphas, with Pilate and Herod, with Festus and Agrippa, with Felix and Gallio, than with St. Paul and the Lord Jesus Christ.

II. I pass on now to the second thing I proposed to speak of. *When is a man truly zealous in religion?*

There never was a grace of which Satan has not made a counterfeit. There never was a good coin issued from the mint, but forgers at once have coined something very like it. It was one of Nero's cruel practices first to sew up Christians in the skins of wild beasts, and then bait them with dogs. It is one of Satan's devices to place distorted copies of the believer's graces before the eyes of men, and so to bring the true graces into contempt. No grace has suffered so much in this way as zeal. Of none perhaps are there so many shams and counterfeits abroad. We must therefore clear the ground of all rubbish on this question. We must find out when zeal in religion is really good, and true, and of God.

(1) Reader, if zeal be true, it will be a *zeal according to knowledge*. It must not be a blind, ignorant zeal. It

must be a calm, reasonable, intelligent principle, which can show the warrant of Scripture for every step it takes. The unconverted Jews had zeal. Paul says, "I bear them record that they have a zeal of God, *but not according to knowledge*" (Rom. 10:2) Saul had zeal when he was a persecuting Pharisee. He says himself, in one of his addresses to the Jews, "I was *zealous* toward God, as ye all are this day" (Acts 22:3). Manasseh had zeal in the days when he was an idolater. The man who made his own children pass through fire, who gave up the fruit of his body to Moloch, to atone for the sin of his soul—that man had zeal. James and John had zeal when they would have called down fire on a Samaritan village. But our Lord rebuked them. Peter had zeal when he drew his sword and cut off the ear of Malchus. But he was quite wrong. Bonner and Gardiner had zeal when they burned Latimer and Cranmer. Were they not in earnest? Let us do them justice. They were zealous, though it was for an unscriptural religion. The members of the inquisition in Spain had zeal, when they tortured men, and put them to horrible deaths, because they would not forsake the gospel. Yes, they marched men and women to the stake in solemn procession, and called it "An Act of Faith," and believed they were doing God service. The Hindus, who used to lie down before the car of Juggernaut, and allow their bodies to be crushed under its wheels—had not they zeal? The Indian widows, who used to burn themselves on the funeral pire of their deceased husbands, the Roman Catholics, who persecuted to death the Vaudois and Albigenses, and cast down men and women from rocks and precipices, because they were heretics—had not they zeal? The Saracens, the Crusaders, the Jesuits, the Anabaptists of Münster, the followers of Joanna Southcote— had they not all zeal? Yes! Yes! I do not deny it. All these had zeal beyond question. They were all zealous. They were all in earnest. But their zeal was not such zeal as God approves—it was not a "zeal according to knowledge."

(2) Furthermore, if zeal be true, it will be a zeal *from true motives*. Such is the subtlety of the heart, that men will often do right things from wrong motives. Amaziah and Joash, kings of Judah, are striking proofs of this. Just so a man may have zeal about things that are good and right, but from second-rate motives, and not from a desire to please God. And such zeal is worth nothing. It is reprobate silver. It is utterly wanting when placed in the balance of God. Man looks only at the actions. God looks at the motives. Man only thinks of the quantity of work done. God considers the doer's heart.

There is such a thing as zeal from *party spirit*. It is quite possible for a man to be unwearied in promoting the interests of his own church or denomination, and yet to have no grace in his own heart, to be ready to die for the peculiar opinions of his own section of Christians, and yet to have no real love to Christ. Such was the zeal of the Pharisees. They "compassed sea and land to make one proselyte, and when he was made, they made him two-fold more the child of hell than themselves" (Matt. 23:15). This zeal is not true.

There is such a thing as zeal from mere *selfishness*. There are times when it is men's interest to be zealous in religion. Power and patronage are sometimes given to godly men. The good things of the world are sometimes to be attained by wearing a cloak of religion. And whenever this is the case, there is no lack of false zeal. Such was the zeal of Joab, when he served David. Such was the zeal of only too many Englishmen in the days of the Commonwealth, when the Puritans were in power.

There is such a thing as zeal from the *love of praise*. Such was the zeal of Jehu, when he was putting down the worship of Baal. Remember how he met Jonadab, the son of Rechab, and said, "Come with me, and see my zeal for the Lord" (II Kings 10:16). Such is the zeal that Bunyan refers to in *Pilgrim's Progress*, when he speaks of some who went "for praise" to Mount Zion. Some people feed on the praise of their fellow creatures. They would rather have it from Christians than have none at all.

Ah, reader, it is a sad and humbling proof of man's corruption, that there is no degree of self-denial and self-sacrifice to which men may not go from false motives. It does not follow that a man's religion is true, because he "gives his body to be burned," or because he gives his "goods to feed the poor." The apostle Paul tells us that a man may do this, and yet not have true charity. It does not follow because men go into a wilderness, and become hermits, that therefore they know what true self-denial is. It does not follow because people immure themselves in monasteries and nunneries, or become sisters of charity, and sisters of mercy, that therefore they know what true crucifixion of the flesh and self-sacrifice is in the sight of God. All these things people may do on wrong principles. They may do them from wrong motives—to satisfy a secret pride and love of notoriety, but not from the true motive of zeal for the glory of God. All such zeal, let us understand, is false. It is of earth, and not of heaven.

(3) Furthermore, if zeal be true, it will be a zeal *about things according to God's mind, and sanctioned by plain examples in God's Word*. Take, for one instance, that highest and best kind of zeal—I mean zeal for our own growth in personal holiness. Such zeal will make a

man feel incessantly that sin is the mightiest of all evils, and conformity to Christ the greatest of all blessings. It will make him feel that there is nothing which ought not to be done, in order to keep up a close walk with God. It will make him willing to cut off the right hand, or pluck out the right eye, or make any sacrifice if only he can attain a closer communion with Jesus. Is not this just what you see in the apostle Paul? He says, "I keep under my body, and bring it into subjection: lest that by any means, when I have preached to others, I myself should be a castaway." "I count not myself to have apprehended: but this one thing I do, forgetting those things which are behind, and reaching forth unto those things which are before, I press toward the mark" (I Cor. 9:27; Phil. 3:13, 14).

Take, for another instance, zeal for the salvation of souls. Such zeal will make a man burn with desire to enlighten the darkness which covers the souls of multitudes, and to bring every man, woman, and child he sees to the knowledge of the gospel. Is not this what you see in the Lord Jesus? It is said that He neither gave Himself, nor His disciples, leisure so much as to eat (Mark 6:31). Is not this what you see in the apostle Paul? He says, "I am made all things to all men, that I might by all means save some" (I Cor. 9:22).

Take, for another instance, zeal against evil practices. Such zeal will make a man hate everything which God hates, and long to sweep it from the face of the earth. It will make him jealous of God's honor and glory, and look on everything which robs Him of it as an offense. Is not this what you see in Phineas, the son of Eleazar? Or in Hezekiah and Josiah, when they put down idolatry?

Take, for another instance, zeal for maintaining the doctrines of the gospel. Such zeal will make a man hate unscriptural teaching, just as he hates sin. It will make him regard religious error as a pestilence which must be checked, whatever may be the cost. It will make him scrupulously careful about every jot and tittle of the counsel of God, lest by some omission the whole gospel should be spoiled. Is not this what you see in Paul at Antioch, when he withstood Peter to the face, and said he was to be blamed? (Gal. 2:11). These are the kind of things about which true zeal is employed. Such zeal, let us understand, is honorable before God.

(4) Furthermore, if zeal be true, it will be a zeal *tempered with charity and love*. It will not be a bitter zeal. It will not be a fierce enmity against persons. It will not be a zeal ready to take the sword, and to smite with carnal weapons. The weapons of true zeal are not carnal, but spiritual. True zeal will hate sin, and yet love the sinner. True zeal will hate heresy, and yet love the heretic. True zeal will long to break the idol, but deeply pity the idolater. True zeal will abhor every kind of wickedness, but labor to do good, even to the vilest of transgressors. True zeal will warn as St. Paul warned the Galatians, and yet feel tenderly as a nurse, or a mother over erring children. It will expose false teachers, as Jesus did the scribes and Pharisees, and yet weep tenderly, as Jesus did over Jerusalem, when He came near to it for the last time. True zeal will be decided as a surgeon dealing with a diseased limb; but true zeal will be gentle as one that is dressing the wounds of a brother. True zeal will speak truth boldly, like Athanasius, against the world, and not care who is offended; but true zeal will endeavor in all its speaking, to speak the truth in love.

(5) Furthermore, if zeal be true, *it will be joined to a deep humility*. A truly zealous man will be the last to discover the greatness of his own attainments. All that he is and does will come so immensely short of his own desires, that he will be filled with a sense of his own

unprofitableness, and amazed to think that God should work by him at all. Like Moses, when he came down from the mount, he will not know that his face shines. Like the righteous, in the twenty-fifth chapter of St. Matthew, he will not be aware of his own good works. Dr. Buchanan is one whose praise is in all the churches. He was one of the first to take up the cause of the perishing heathen. He literally spent himself, body and mind, in laboring to arouse sleeping Christians to see the importance of missions. Yet he says in one of his letters, "I do not know that I ever had what Christians call zeal." Whitefield was one of the most zealous preachers of the gospel the world has ever seen. Fervent in spirit, instant in season and out of season, he was a burning and a shining light, and turned thousands to God. Yet he says, after preaching for thirty years, "Lord help me to begin to begin." McCheyne was one of the greatest blessings that God ever gave to the Church of Scotland. He was a minister insatiably desirous of the salvation of souls. Few men ever did so much good as he did, though he died at the age of twenty-nine. Yet he says in one of his letters, "None but God knows what an abyss of corruption is in my heart. It is perfectly wonderful that ever God could bless such a ministry." Ah, reader, where there is self-conceit, there is little true zeal!

Reader, I ask you particularly to remember the description of true zeal, which I have just given. Zeal according to knowledge, zeal from true motives, zeal warranted by scriptural examples, zeal tempered with charity, zeal accompanied by deep humility—this is true genuine zeal, this is the kind of zeal which God approves. Of such zeal, you and I never need fear having too much.

I ask you to remember the description, because of the times in which you live. Beware of supposing that sincerity alone can ever make up true zeal, that earnestness, however ignorant, makes a man a really zealous Christian in the sight of God. There is a generation in these days which makes an idol of what it is pleased to call *"earnestness"* in religion. These men will allow no fault to be found with an *"earnest man."* Whatever his theological opinions may be, if he be but an earnest man, that is enough for these people, and we are to ask no more. They tell you we have nothing to do with minute points of doctrine, and with questions of words and names, about which Chrisitans are not agreed. Is the man an earnest man? If he is, we ought to be satisfied. Earnestness in their eyes covers over a multitude of sins. I warn you solemnly to beware of this specious doctrine. In the name of the gospel, and in the name of the Bible, I enter my protest against the theory, that mere earnestness can make a man a truly zealous and pious man in the sight of God.

These idolaters of earnestness would make out that God has given us no standard of truth and error, or that the true standard, the Bible, is so obscure, that no man can find out what truth is by simply going to it. They pour contempt upon the Word, the written Word, and therefore they must be wrong.

These idolaters of earnestness would make us condemn every witness for the truth, and every opponent of false teaching, from the time of the Lord Jesus down to this day. The scribes and Pharisees were in earnest, and yet our Lord opposed them. And shall we dare even to hint a suspicion that they ought to have been let alone? Queen Mary, and Bonner, and Gardiner were in earnest in restoring popery, and trying to put down Protestantism, and yet Ridley and Latimer opposed them to the death. And shall we dare to say that as both parties were in earnest, both were in the right? Devil-worshipers and idolaters at this day are in earnest, and yet our missionaries labor to expose their errors. And shall we dare to say that earnestness would take them to heaven, and that missionaries to heathen and Roman Catholics had better stay at home? Are we really going to admit that the Bible does not show us what is truth? Are we really going to put a mere vague thing called "earnestness," in the place of Christ, and to maintain that no earnest man can be wrong? God forbid that we should give place to such doctrine! I shrink with horror from such theology. I warn you solemnly to beware of being carried away by it, for it is common and most seductive in this day. Beware of it, for it is only a new form of an old error—that old error which says that a man "Can't be wrong whose life is in the right." Admire zeal. Seek after zeal. Encourage zeal. But see that your own zeal be true. See that the zeal, which you admire in others, be a zeal "according to knowledge," a zeal from right motives, a zeal that can bring chapter and verse out of the Bible for its foundation. Any zeal but this is but a false fire. It is not lighted by the Holy Ghost.

III. I pass on now to the third thing I proposed to speak of. Let me show you *why it is good for a man to be zealous*.

It is certain that God never gave a man a commandment which it was not man's interest, as well as duty, to obey. He never set a grace before His believing people which His people will not find it their highest happiness to follow after. This is true of all the graces of the Christian character. Perhaps it is preeminently true in the case of zeal.

Zeal is *good for a Christian's own soul*. We all know that exercise is good for the health, and that regular employment of our muscles and limbs promotes our bodily comfort, and increases our bodily vigor. Now that which exercise does for our bodies, zeal will do for our souls. It will help mightily to promote inward feelings of joy, peace, comfort, and happiness. None have so much enjoyment of Christ as those who are ever zealous for His glory, jealous over their own walk, tender over their own consciences, full of anxiety about the souls of others, and ever watching, working, laboring, striving, and toiling to extend the knowledge of Jesus Christ upon earth. Such men live in the full light of the sun, and therefore their hearts are always warm. Such men water others, and therefore they are watered themselves. Their hearts are like a garden daily refreshed by the dew of the Holy Ghost. They honor God, and so God honors them.

I would not be mistaken in saying this. I would not appear to speak slightingly of any believer. I know that the Lord takes pleasure in all His people. There is not one, from the least to the greatest, from the smallest child in the kingdom of God, to the oldest warrior in the battle against Satan—there is not one in whom the Lord Jesus Christ does not take great pleasure. We are all His children; and however weak and feeble some of us may be, as a father pitieth his children, so does the Lord pity them that love and fear Him. We are all plants of His own planting; and though many of us are poor, weakly exotics, scarcely keeping life together in a foreign soil, yet as the gardener loves that which his hands have reared, so does the Lord Jesus love the poor sinners that trust in Him. But while I say this, I do also believe that the Lord takes special pleasure in those who are zealous for Him, in those who give themselves, body, soul and spirit, to extend His glory in this world. To them He reveals Himself, as He does not to others. To them He shows things that other men never see. He blesses the work of their hands. He cheers them with spiritual consolations, which others only know by the hearing of the ear. They are men after His own heart, for they are men more like Himself than others. None have such joy and peace in believing, none have such sensible comfort in their religion, none have so much of heaven upon earth, none see and feel so much of the consolations of the gospel as those who are zealous, earnest, thorough-going, devoted Christians. For the sake of our own souls, if there were no other reason, it is good to be zealous—to be very zealous in our religion.

Reader, as zeal is good for ourselves individually, so it is also *good for the professing church of Christ generally*. Nothing so much keeps alive true religion as a leaven of zealous Christians scattered to and fro throughout a church. Like salt, they prevent the whole body falling into a state of corruption. None but men of this kind can revive churches when ready to die. It is impossible to overestimate the debt that all Christians owe to zeal. The greatest mistake the rulers of a church can make, is to drive zealous men out of its pale. By so doing, they drain out the lifeblood of the system, and hasten on ecclesiastical decline and death.

Zeal is in truth that grace which God seems to delight to honor. Look through the list of Christians who have been eminent for usefulness. Who are the men that have left the deepest and most indelible marks on the church of their day? Who are the men that God has generally honored to build up the walls of His Zion, and turn the battle from the gate? Not so much men of learning and literary talents, as men of zeal.

Bishop Latimer was not such a deeply read scholar as Cranmer or Ridley. He could not quote Fathers from memory as they did. He refused to be drawn into arguments about antiquity. He stuck to his Bible. Yet it is not too much to say that no English Reformer made such a lasting impression on the nation as old Latimer did. And what was the reason? His simple zeal.

Baxter, the Puritan, was not equal to some of his con-
temporaries in intellectual gifts. It is no disparagement
to say that he does not stand on a level with Manton or
Owen. Yet few men probably exercised so wide an influence on the generation in which he lived. And what was
the reason? His burning zeal.

Whitefield, and Wesley, and Berridge, and Venn
were inferior in mental attainments to Bishops Butler
and Watson. But they produced effects on the people of
this country which fifty Butlers and Watsons would
probably never have produced. They saved the Church
of England from ruin. And what was one secret of their
power? Their zeal.

These men stood forward at turning points in the
history of the church. They bore unmoved storms of
opposition and persecution. They were not afraid to
stand alone. They cared not though their motives were
misinterpreted. They counted all things but loss for the
truth's sake. They were each and all and every one eminently *men of one thing*—and that one thing was to advance the glory of God, and to maintain His truth in the
world. They were all fire, and so they lighted others.
They were wide awake, and so they awakened others.
They were all alive, and so they quickened others. They
were always working, and so they shamed others into
working too. They came down upon men like Moses
from the mount. They shone as if they had been in the
presence of God. They carried to and fro with them, as
they walked their course through the world, something
of the atmosphere and savor of heaven itself.

There is a sense in which it may be said that zeal is
contagious. Nothing is more useful to the professors of
Christianity than to see a real live Christian—a thoroughly zealous man of God. They may rail at him. They
may carp at him. They may pick holes in his conduct.

They may look shy upon him. They may not understand him any more than men understand a new comet, when a new comet appears; but insensibly a zealous man does them good. He opens their eyes. He makes them feel their own sleepiness. He makes their own great darkness visible. He obliges them to see their own barrenness. He compels them to think, whether they like it or not, "What are we doing? Are we no better than mere cumberers of the ground?" It may be sadly true that "one sinner *destroyeth* much good!" But it is also a blessed truth that one zealous Christian can *do* much good. Yes, one single zealous man in a town, one zealous man in a congregation, one zealous man in a society, one zealous man in a family, may be a great, a most extensive blessing. How many machines of usefulness such a man sets a going! How much Christian activity he often calls into being which would otherwise have slept! How many fountains he opens which would otherwise have been sealed! Verily there is a deep mine of truth in those words of the apostle Paul to the Corinthians, "Your zeal hath provoked very many" (II Cor. 9:2).

But, as zeal is good for the church and for individuals, so zeal is *good for the world*. Where would the missonary work be if it were not for zeal? Where would our city missions and ragged schools be if it were not for zeal? Where would our district-visiting and pastoral-aid societies be if it were not for zeal? Where would be our societies for rooting out sin and ignorance, for finding out the dark places of the earth, and recovering poor lost souls? Where would be all these glorious instruments for good if it were not for Christian zeal? Zeal called these institutions into being, and zeal keeps them at work when they have begun. Zeal gathers a few despised men, and makes them the nucleus of many a powerful society. Zeal keeps up the collections of a society when it is formed. Zeal prevents men from becoming lazy and sleepy when the machine has grown large, and begins to get favor from the world. Zeal raises up men to go forth, putting their lives in their hands, like Moffat and Williams in our own day. Zeal supplies their place when they are gathered into the garner, and raises up a constant succession of laborers to do the Lord's work.

What would become of the ignorant masses who crowd the lanes and alleys of overgrown cities, if it were not for Christian zeal? Governments can do nothing with them: they cannot make laws that will meet the evil. The vast majority of professing Christians have no eyes to see it; like the priest and Levite, they pass by on the other side. But zeal has eyes to see, and a heart to feel, and a head to devise, and a tongue to plead, and hands to work, and feet to travel, in order to rescue poor souls, and raise them from their low estate. Zeal does not stand poring over difficulties, but simply says, "Here are souls perishing, and something *shall* be done." Zeal does not shrink back because there are Anakims in the way: it looks over their heads, like Moses on Pisgah, and says, "The land *shall* be possessed." Zeal does not wait for company, and tarry till good works are fashionable: it goes forward like a forlorn hope, and trusts that others will follow by and by. Ah, reader, the world little knows what a debt it owes to Christian zeal! How much crime it has checked! How much sedition it has prevented! How much public discontent it has calmed! How much obedience to law and love of order it has produced! How many souls it has saved! Yes, and I believe we little know what might be done if every Christian was a zealous man. How much if ministers were more like Bickersteth, and Whitefield, and McCheyne! How much if layman were more like Howard, and Wilberforce, and Thornton, and Nasmith!

Oh, for the world's sake, as well as your own, resolve, labor, strive to be zealous Christians!

Beware, I beseech you, of checking zeal. Seek it. Cultivate it. Try to blow up the fire in your own heart, and the hearts of others, but never, never check it. Beware of throwing cold water on zealous souls, whenever you meet with them. Beware of nipping in the bud this precious grace when first it shoots. If you are a parent, beware of checking it in your children; if you are a husband, beware of checking it in your wife; if you are a brother, beware of checking it in your sisters; and if you are a minister, beware of checking it in the members of your congregation. It is a shoot of heaven's own planting. Beware of crushing it, for Christ's sake. Zeal may make mistakes. Zeal may need directing. Zeal may want guiding, controlling, and advising. Like the elephants on ancient fields of battle, it may sometimes do injury to its own side. But zeal does not need damping in a wretched, cold, corrupt, miserable world like this. Zeal, like John Knox pulling down the Scotch monasteries, may hurt the feelings of narrow-minded and sleepy Christians. It may offend the prejudices of those old-fashioned religionists, who hate everything new, and abhor all change. But zeal in the end will be justified by its results. Zeal, like John Knox, in the long run of life, will do infinitely more good than harm. Oh, reader, there is little danger of there being too much zeal for the glory of God. God forgive those who think there is! You know little of human nature. You forget that sickness is far more contagious than health, and that it is much easier to catch a cold than impart a glow. Depend upon it, the church seldom needs a bridle, but often needs a spur. It seldom needs to be checked, but often needs to be urged on.

And now, in conclusion, let me try to apply this subject to the conscience of every person who reads this volume. It is a warning subject, an arousing subject, an encouraging subject, according to the state of our several hearts. I wish by God's help to give every reader his portion.

(1) First of all let me offer *a warning* to all who make no decided profession of religion. There are thousands and tens of thousands, I fear, in this condition. Reader, if you are one, the subject before you is full of solemn warning. Oh, that the Lord in mercy may incline your heart to receive it!

I ask you then in all affection, Where is your zeal in religion? With the Bible before me, I may well be bold in asking. But with your life before me, I may well tremble as to the answer. I ask again, Where is your zeal for the glory of God? Where is your zeal for extending Christ's gospel through an evil world? Zeal, which was the characteristic of the Lord Jesus—zeal, which is the characteristic of the angels—zeal, which shines forth in all the brightest Christians; where is your zeal, unconverted reader, where is your zeal indeed? You know well it is nowhere at all. You know well you see no beauty in it. You know well it is scorned and cast out as evil by you and your companions. You know well it has no place, no portion, no standing ground, in the religion of you soul. It is not that you know not what it is to be zealous. You have zeal, but it is all misapplied. It is all earthly. It is all about the things of time. It is not zeal for the glory of God. It is not zeal for the salvation of souls. Yes, many a man has zeal for the newspaper, but not for the Bible; zeal for the daily reading of the "Times," but no zeal for the daily reading of God's blessed Word. Many a man has zeal for the account book and the business book, but no zeal about the Book of Life, and the last great account; zeal about Australian and Californian gold, but no zeal about the unsearchable riches of Christ. Many a man has zeal about his earthly concerns—his family, his pleasures, his daily pursuits; but no zeal about God, and heaven, and eternity.

Reader, if this is your case, awake, I do beseech you, to see your gross *folly*. You cannot live forever. You are not ready to die. You are utterly unfit for the company of saints and angels. Awake! Be zealous and repent. Awake to see the *harm* you are doing. You are putting arguments in the hands of infidels by your shameful coldness. You are pulling down as fast as ministers build. You are helping the devil. Awake! Be zealous and repent. Awake to see your childish *inconsistency*. What can be more worthy of zeal than eternal things, than the glory of God, than the salvation of souls? Surely if it is good to labor for rewards that are temporal, it is a thousand times better to labor for those that are eternal. Awake! Be zealous and repent. Go and read that long-neglected Bible. Take up that blessed Book which you have, and perhaps never use. Read that New Testament through. Do you find nothing there to make you zealous, to make you earnest about your soul? Go and look at the cross of Christ. Go and see how the Son of God there shed His precious blood for you, how He suffered and groaned, and died for you, how He poured out His soul as an offering for sin, in order that you, sinful brother or sister, might not perish, but have eternal life. Go and look at the cross of Christ, and never rest till you feel some zeal for your own soul, some zeal for the glory of God, some zeal for extension of the gospel throughout the world.

(2) Let me, in the next place, say something *to arouse* those who make a profession of being decided Christians, and are yet lukewarm in their practice. There are only too many, I regret to say, in this state of soul. Reader, if you are one, there is much in this subject which ought to lead you to searchings of heart.

Let me speak to your conscience. To you also I desire to put the question in all brotherly affection, Where is your zeal? Where is your zeal for the glory of God, and for extending the gospel throughout the world? You know well it is very low. You know well that your zeal is a little feeble glimmering spark, that just lives, and no more; it is like a thing ready to die. Surely there is a fault somewhere, if this is the case. This state of things ought not to be. You, the child of God—you, redeemed at so glorious a price—you, ransomed with such precious blood—you, who are an heir of glory such as no tongue ever yet told, or eye saw; surely you ought to be a man of another kind. Surely your zeal ought not to be so small.

I deeply feel that this is a painful subject to touch upon. I do it with reluctance, and with a constant remembrance of my own unprofitableness. Nevertheless truth ought to be spoken. The plain truth is, that many believers in the present day seem so dreadfully afraid of doing harm that they hardly ever dare to do good. There are many who are fruitful in objections, but barren in actions; rich in wet blankets, but poor in anything like Christian fire. They are like the Dutch deputies who would never allow Marlborough to venture anything, and by their excessive caution prevented many a victory being won. Truly, in looking round the church of Christ, a man might sometimes think that God's kingdom had come, and God's will was being done upon earth, so small is the zeal that some believers show. It is

vain to deny it. I need not go far for evidence. I point to
societies for doing good to the heathen, the colonies,
and the dark places of our own land, languishing and
standing still for want of active support. I ask *is this zeal?*
I point to thousands of miserable guinea subscriptions
which are never missed by the givers, and yet make up
the sum of their Christian liberality. I ask *is this real?* I
point to false doctrine allowed to grow up in parishes
and families without an effort being made to check it,
while so-called believers look on, and content themselves with wishing it was not so. I ask *is this zeal?*
Would the apostles have been satisfied with such a state
of things? We know they would not.

Reader, if your conscience pleads guilty to any par-
ticipation in the shortcomings I have spoken of, I call
upon you, in the name of the Lord, to awake, be
zealous, and repent. Let not zeal be confined to
Lincoln's Inn, the Temple, and Westminster; to banks,
and shops, and countinghouses. Let us see the same zeal
in the church of Christ. Let not zeal be abundant to get
gold from Australia, and rescue Franklin from thick-
ribbed ice, but defective to send the gospel to the
heathen, or to pluck Roman Catholics like brands from
the fire, or to enlighten the dark places of the colonies of
this great land. Never were there such doors of usefulness opened, never were there so many opportunities for
doing good. I loathe that squeamishness which refuses
to help religious works if there is a blemish about the instrument by which the work is carried on. At this rate we
might never do anything at all. Resist the feeling,
reader, if you are tempted by it. It is one of Satan's
devices. It is better to work with feeble instruments than
not to work at all. At all events, try to do something for
God and Christ—something against ignorance and sin.
Give, collect, teach, exhort, visit, pray, according as

God enables you. Only make up your mind that all can do something, and resolve that by you, at any rate, something shall be done. If you have only one talent, do not bury it in the ground. Try to live so as to be missed. There is far more to be done in twelve hours than most of us have ever yet done on any day in our lives.

Think of the *precious souls* which are perishing, while you are sleeping. Be taken up with your inward conflicts if you will. Go on anatomizing your own feelings, and poring over your own corruptions, if you are so determined. But remember all this time souls are going to hell, and you might do something to save them by working, by giving, by writing, by begging, and by prayer. Oh, awake, be zealous and repent.

Think of the *shortness of time*. You will soon be gone. You will have no opportunity for works of mercy in another world. In heaven there will be no ignorant people to instruct, and no unconverted to reclaim. Whatever you do must be done now. Oh, when are you going to begin? Awake! Be zealous and repent.

Think of *the devil,* and his zeal to do harm. It was a solemn saying of Old Bernard when he said that "Satan would rise up in judgment against some people at the last day, because he had shown more zeal to ruin souls than they had to save them." Awake! Be zealous and repent.

Think of *your Savior,* and all His zeal for you. Think of Him in Gethsemane and on Calvary, shedding His blood for sinners. Think of His life and death, His sufferings and His doings. This He has done for you. What are you doing for Him? Oh, resolve that for the time to come you will spend and be spent for Christ! Awake! Be zealous and repent.

(3) Last of all let me encourage all readers of these pages who are truly zealous Christians.

I have but one request to make, and that is *that you will persevere*. I do beseech you to hold fast your zeal, and never let it go. I do beseech you never to go back from your first works, never to leave your first love, never to let it be said of you that your first things were better than your last. Beware of cooling down. You have only to be lazy and sit still, and you will soon lose all your warmth. You will soon become another man from what you are now. Oh, reader, do not think this a needless exhortation.

It may be very true that wise young believers are very rare. But it is no less true that zealous old believers are very rare also. Never allow yourself to think that you can do too much, that you can spend and be spent too much for Christ's cause. For one man that does too much I will show you a thousand who do not do enough. Rather think that the night cometh, when no man can work—and give, collect, teach, visit, work, pray, as if you were doing it for the last time. Lay to heart the words of that noble-minded Jansenist, who said when told that he ought to rest a little, "What should we rest for? Have we not all eternity to rest in?"

Fear not the reproach of men. Faint not because you are sometimes abused. Heed it not if you are sometimes called bigot, enthusiast, fanatic, madman, and fool. There is nothing disgraceful in these titles. They have often been given to the best and wisest of men. If you are only to be zealous when you are praised for it, if the wheels of your zeal must be oiled by the world's commendation, your zeal will be but short-lived. Care not for the praise or frown of man. There is but one thing worth caring for, and that is the praise of God. There is but one question worth asking about our actions: "How will they look in the day of judgment?"

Reader, I lay these thoughts before you, and I ask you seriously to consider them.

If you are not yet a zealous man, I pray that God may make you one. If you are, I pray that your zeal may increase more and more to your life's end.

PROPHECY

BY

J. C. RYLE

In a courteous yet vigorous manner J. C. Ryle examines different interpretations of Biblical prophecy and proceeds to give Scriptural advice to believers regarding what can sometimes be a difficult and confusing subject.

Although first written over a century ago, this book is relevant for today. Indeed some of the prophecies that Ryle focuses on have been fulfilled and this should encourage Christians to believe God's Word.

Ryle, in this volume, particularly addresses two areas. He describes the duty of believers as they anticipate their Lord's return and he expounds the Bible's predictions regarding the nation of Israel.

Today much prophetic literature is sensational and has often turned out to be wrong. In contrast, Ryle's book is sane and thought-provoking.

pocket   paperback

256 pages

ISBN 1 876 676 649

IN LARGE PRINT
BY
J. C. RYLE

(1) ASSURANCE

Ryle in a lucid manner examines the Biblical grounds for believers enjoying assurance of God's grace and explains how assurance can be experienced.

pocket paperback

160 pages   ISBN 1 871676 05 6

(2) HEAVEN

In his warm personal style, Ryle encourages us to look forward to heaven, to a reunion with old friends and to being with our Father for ever.

pocket paperback

96 pages   ISBN I 871676 75 4